Padua Travel

Explore the Scrovegni Chapel, Basilica of Saint Anthony, and Prato Della Valle—Your Complete Guide to Italy's Historic City

Feranmi Samuel

Copyright © 2024 by Feranmi Samuel

All rights reserved.

No part of this publication may be reproduced, stored or transmitted in any form or by any means, electronic, mechanical, photocopying, recording, scanning, or otherwise without written permission from the publisher. It is illegal to copy this book, post it to a website, or distribute it by any other means without permission. Feranmi Samuel asserts the moral right to be identified as the author of this work.

Contents

Chapter 1: Introduction

Welcome to Padua

Historical Overview

Cultural Significance

How to Use This Guide

Quick Facts and Figures

Chapter 2: Planning Your Trip

Best Time to Visit

Travel Documents and Visas

Getting to Padua

Getting Around Padua

Travel Tips and Etiquette

Chapter 3: Where to Stay

Luxury Hotels

Mid-Range Hotels

Budget Accommodations

Unique Stays: B&Bs and Boutique Hotels

Family-Friendly Accommodations

Chapter 4: Top Tourist Attractions

Basilica of Saint Anthony

Scrovegni Chapel

Prato della Valle

Palazzo della Ragione

Botanical Garden of Padua

Piazza dei Signori

Padua Cathedral

University of Padua and the Anatomical Theatre

Musei Civici agli Eremitani

Orto Botanico di Padova

Chapter 5: Exploring Padua's Neighborhoods

Historic City Center

The University District

Jewish Ghetto

Portello District

Arcella Neighborhood

Around Prato della Valle

Chapter 6: Dining and Cuisine

Traditional Padua Dishes

Best Restaurants for Fine Dining

Casual and Budget Eats

Street Food and Local Markets

Cafes and Gelaterias

Vegetarian and Vegan Options

Chapter 7: Shopping in Padua

Markets and Bazaars

Local Artisan Shops

Souvenirs and Gifts

Shopping Malls and Outlets

Chapter 8: Arts, Culture, and Entertainment

Theaters and Concert Halls

Museums and Art Galleries

Festivals and Events

Nightlife and Bars

    Cinema and Performing Arts

    Music and Dance

Chapter 9: Outdoor Activities and Nature

    Parks and Gardens

    Walking and Cycling Tours

    Day Trips and Excursions

    Boating on the River Bacchiglione

    Sports and Recreation

Chapter 10: Itineraries for Every Traveler

    Weekend Getaway

    Family-Friendly Itinerary

    Romantic Retreat

    Cultural Enthusiast

    Outdoor Adventure

    Food and Wine Lover

    Budget Traveler

    Returning Visitor Highlights

Chapter 11: Practical Information

Health and Safety

Emergency Contacts

Local Customs and Etiquette

Currency and Banking

Language and Communication

Chapter 12: Day Trips from Padua

Venice

Verona

Vicenza

Treviso

The Euganean Hills

Chapter 13: Tips for Sustainable Travel

Eco-Friendly Accommodations

Sustainable Dining

Responsible Tourism Practices

Supporting Local Businesses

Conclusion

Appendix

Useful Apps and Websites

Further Reading and References

Contact Information for Tourism Offices

Padua Map

Chapter 1: Introduction

Welcome to Padua

Exploring Padua was a journey that truly captivated my heart and soul. As a professional travel guide writer, I've roamed the bustling streets of Tokyo, traversed the serene landscapes of the Dolomites, and savored the vibrant culture of Mexico. Yet, Padua offered something uniquely enchanting, a blend of history, art, and Italian charm that made it stand out among the many places I've been fortunate enough to visit.

It all started with a morning stroll through the Prato della Valle, one of Europe's largest squares. The sunlight danced on the surface of the central elliptical island, surrounded by a moat adorned with statues of Padua's most notable figures. The sight was both majestic and calming, a perfect introduction to the city's grandeur. As I wandered through the square, I couldn't help but feel a sense of anticipation, knowing that Padua had so much more to reveal.

My adventure continued at the Basilica of Saint Anthony. The basilica's grandeur and spiritual aura were palpable as I stepped inside. The walls echoed with centuries of prayers and devotion, and the artistry of the frescoes and statues left me in awe. It was a place where history and faith intertwined seamlessly, providing a profound experience that resonated deeply with me.

The Scrovegni Chapel was another highlight of my journey. As an art enthusiast, seeing Giotto's frescoes in person was a dream come true. The vivid colors and emotional depth of his work transported me back to the 14th century, allowing me to appreciate the beauty and significance of his contributions to the art world. It was a reminder of the timeless power of art to move and inspire us.

Padua's University, one of the oldest in the world, offered a different kind of allure. Walking through its historic halls and visiting the Anatomical Theatre, I felt connected to the countless scholars and thinkers who had studied there. It was fascinating to imagine the intellectual fervor that once filled these spaces, contributing to advancements in science, medicine, and philosophy.

But Padua isn't just about grand historical sites and artistic masterpieces. The city's vibrant street life, cozy cafes, and bustling markets offered a warm and welcoming atmosphere. I found joy in simple pleasures, like sipping an espresso at a local cafe, chatting with friendly locals, and exploring charming artisan shops. These everyday experiences added a rich layer to my understanding of Padua, revealing its true spirit and character.

Writing this travel guide has been a labor of love, driven by a desire to share the magic of Padua with others. Whether you're planning your first visit or returning for another adventure, this guide is crafted to help you uncover the city's hidden gems and make the most of your stay. With detailed itineraries, insider tips, and a deep appreciation for Padua's cultural heritage, this book is your passport to an unforgettable journey.

So why should you read my book? Because it's more than

just a travel guide. It's a narrative of discovery, a celebration of Padua's beauty, and an invitation to experience the city through the eyes of someone who has fallen in love with it. Join me on this adventure, and let's explore the wonders of Padua together.

Historical Overview

Padua is one of those cities that whispers tales of centuries past at every turn. Walking through its cobblestone streets, I felt as if I was stepping back in time. Nestled in the Veneto region of Northern Italy, Padua boasts a history that spans over 3,000 years. Its origins date back to the Roman era, when it was known as Patavium. As I wandered through the city, I could almost picture the ancient Romans strolling along the same paths.

One of the most remarkable chapters in Padua's history unfolded during the Renaissance. The city became a beacon of learning and culture, attracting scholars and artists from all over Europe. The University of Padua, founded in 1222, played a pivotal role in this intellectual blossoming. It was fascinating to visit the university and imagine the great minds that once walked its halls, including the renowned astronomer Galileo Galilei.

The medieval heart of Padua is dominated by the Basilica of Saint Anthony. Completed in 1310, this architectural marvel draws pilgrims from around the world. The basilica's stunning blend of Romanesque, Gothic, and Byzantine elements is a testament to the city's rich architectural heritage. As I stood before its grandeur, I felt a profound connection to the generations of people who have found solace and inspiration within its walls.

The Scrovegni Chapel is another historical gem that left me awe-struck. Commissioned by the wealthy Scrovegni family in the early 14th century, the chapel is adorned with breathtaking frescoes by Giotto. These vivid paintings depict scenes from the lives of Christ and the Virgin Mary, bringing the stories to life in a way that words alone cannot. Standing in the chapel, surrounded by Giotto's masterpieces, I felt an overwhelming sense of reverence for the artistry and devotion that created this timeless work.

As the centuries passed, Padua continued to evolve, playing a crucial role in the Venetian Republic. The city's strategic location made it a vital hub for trade and commerce. The influence of Venice is evident in Padua's architecture, with elegant palaces and grand squares that mirror the opulence of the Venetian Republic. Walking through these historic sites, I couldn't help but admire the resilience and adaptability of Padua's people, who have preserved their heritage while embracing the future.

Cultural Significance

Padua is a city where culture thrives in every corner. From its vibrant arts scene to its cherished traditions, the city offers a rich tapestry of experiences that captivate both the mind and the heart. One of the things that struck me most about Padua is its deep appreciation for the arts. The city is home to numerous museums and galleries that showcase a wide range of artistic expressions, from classical to contemporary.

The Musei Civici agli Eremitani is a must-visit for any art lover. Housed in a former monastery, this museum complex features an impressive collection of art and archaeology. I spent hours exploring its galleries, marveling at works by Titian, Tintoretto, and other masters. The museum also houses the remnants of the ancient Roman amphitheater, providing a fascinating glimpse into Padua's past.

The University of Padua continues to be a cultural powerhouse, fostering innovation and creativity. Its botanical garden, the Orto Botanico di Padova, is the oldest academic garden in the world, established in 1545. Walking through its serene pathways, I felt a sense of tranquility and wonder at the diversity of plant life. The garden is a living testament to the university's commitment to education and research, offering a peaceful retreat in the heart of the city.

Padua's cultural significance extends beyond the arts to its vibrant festivals and events. One of the highlights of my visit was the Festa di Sant'Antonio, a grand celebration in honor of the city's patron saint. The streets came alive with processions, music, and food stalls, creating a joyous atmosphere that brought the community together. Participating in this festival gave me a deeper appreciation for the city's traditions and the strong sense of identity that unites its people.

The city's culinary culture is another aspect that left a lasting impression on me. Padua's cuisine is a delightful blend of local flavors and Venetian influences. I savored dishes like bigoli in salsa, a thick spaghetti served with a savory anchovy sauce, and risotto alla padovana, a creamy rice dish with chicken livers and spices. Dining in Padua is not just about the food; it's about the experience of sharing a meal with friends and family, enjoying the warmth and hospitality that are hallmarks of Italian culture.

How to Use This Guide

When I set out to write this guide, my goal was to create a resource that would make your journey through Padua as enriching and enjoyable as possible. Whether you're a first-time visitor or a returning traveler, this guide is designed to help you uncover the city's hidden gems and make the most of your stay.

Start by familiarizing yourself with the city's layout. Padua is a city best explored on foot, and its compact size makes it easy to navigate. The historic center, with its narrow streets and picturesque squares, is where you'll find most of the major attractions. Use the detailed maps included in this guide to plan your routes and discover lesser-known neighborhoods that offer their own unique charms.

Each chapter of this guide focuses on a different aspect of

Padua, from its rich history and cultural significance to practical tips for getting around. The itineraries provided will help you tailor your visit to your interests and schedule. Whether you have a weekend or a week, you'll find suggestions for how to spend your time in a way that maximizes your experience.

Be sure to take advantage of the insider tips scattered throughout the guide. These nuggets of wisdom come from my own experiences and the insights of locals who know the city best. From the best times to visit popular attractions to recommendations for off-the-beaten-path spots, these tips will help you experience Padua like a true insider.

As you explore the city, don't be afraid to venture beyond the main tourist sites. Some of my most memorable experiences in Padua came from simply wandering and letting curiosity guide me. Whether it's stumbling upon a hidden courtyard, discovering a charming cafe, or chatting with a friendly local, these spontaneous moments often lead to the most rewarding adventures.

Quick Facts and Figures

Here are some quick facts and figures to help you get acquainted with Padua:

- **Location:** Padua is located in the Veneto region of Northern Italy, approximately 40 kilometers west of Venice.

- **Population:** The city has a population of around 210,000 residents.

- **Language:** Italian is the official language, but many locals speak English, especially in tourist areas.

- **Currency:** The currency used in Padua is the Euro (€).

- **Time Zone:** Padua operates on Central European Time (CET), which is UTC+1. During daylight saving time, it switches to Central European Summer Time (CEST), which is UTC+2.

- **Climate:** Padua has a humid subtropical climate, with hot summers and mild winters. The best times to visit are spring (April to June) and autumn (September to October) when the weather is pleasant and the city is less crowded.

- **Transportation:** Padua is well-connected by train, making it easy to travel to and from other major cities in Italy. The local public transportation system includes buses and trams, which are convenient for getting around the city.

- **Electricity:** The standard voltage is 230V, and the frequency is 50Hz. Power outlets typically accept Type C, F, and L plugs.

- **Emergency Numbers:** The emergency number for police, fire, and medical assistance in Italy is 112.

Padua is a city that offers a perfect blend of history, culture, and modern amenities. Whether you're drawn to its ancient ruins, artistic treasures, or lively street scenes, there's something here for every traveler. I hope this guide serves as a valuable companion on your journey, helping you to discover the many wonders of Padua and create memories that will last a lifetime.

Chapter 2: Planning Your Trip

Planning a trip to Padua is like preparing for an adventure through history, art, and culture. As someone who has spent ample time exploring this fascinating city, I'm excited to share some insights to help you make the most of your journey. Let's dive into the essential details you need to plan your perfect trip to Padua.

Best Time to Visit

Choosing the right time to visit Padua can make a big difference in your experience. The city has a humid subtropical climate, which means hot summers and mild winters. The best times to visit are spring (April to June) and autumn (September to October). During these months, the weather is pleasant, and the city is less crowded with tourists.

Spring in Padua is magical. The city comes to life with blooming flowers and lush greenery, making it a perfect time for leisurely strolls through the Prato della Valle or the Botanical Garden. The temperatures range from 10°C (50°F) to 20°C (68°F), providing a comfortable climate for exploring the city's outdoor attractions.

Autumn is another fantastic season to visit. The weather remains mild, with temperatures ranging from 10°C (50°F) to 18°C (64°F). The fall colors add a picturesque touch to the cityscape, and you'll find plenty of cultural events and festivals taking place. Plus, autumn is harvest season, so you'll have the chance to enjoy fresh local produce and seasonal dishes.

Summer can be quite hot, with temperatures often exceeding 30°C (86°F). However, if you don't mind the heat, this is when the city hosts numerous outdoor events, concerts, and festivals. Just be prepared for larger crowds and higher prices for accommodation.

Winter in Padua is relatively mild, with temperatures rarely dropping below 0°C (32°F). While it's not the most popular time for tourists, the city's charm is still very much present. If you prefer a quieter, more relaxed visit, winter might be a good option. Plus, you'll get to experience the local holiday traditions and decorations.

Travel Documents and Visas

Before you pack your bags, it's important to ensure you have all the necessary travel documents. If you're a citizen of the European Union (EU), you won't need a visa to enter Italy. Just bring your passport or national ID card.

For travelers from the United States, Canada, Australia, and several other countries, you can enter Italy without a visa for up to 90 days within a 180-day period for tourism purposes. All you need is a valid passport that remains valid for at least three months beyond your intended stay.

If you're coming from a country that requires a visa to enter Italy, be sure to apply well in advance. The process typically involves filling out an application form, providing proof of accommodation and financial means, and attending an interview at your nearest Italian consulate or embassy. It's also a good idea to check the latest entry requirements on the official Italian government website or with your local embassy, as regulations can change.

Regardless of where you're from, always carry a copy of your passport and important documents in case of emergencies. It's also helpful to have digital copies stored securely online.

Getting to Padua

Padua is conveniently located in Northern Italy, making it easily accessible from various parts of the country and Europe. The city doesn't have its own airport, but it's well-connected to major airports in the region.

The nearest major airport is Venice Marco Polo Airport (VCE), which is about 40 kilometers (25 miles) away. From the airport, you can take a shuttle bus, which runs frequently and takes about an hour to reach Padua. Alternatively, you can catch a train from Venice Mestre station, which is connected to the airport by bus or taxi.

Another option is the Treviso Airport (TSF), approximately 60 kilometers (37 miles) from Padua. This airport mainly serves budget airlines, so it might be a good choice if you're looking for cheaper flights. From Treviso, you can take a bus or taxi to the train station and then hop on a train to Padua.

If you're traveling by train, Padua is a major stop on the Italian railway network. High-speed trains connect Padua to cities like Milan, Florence, Rome, and Bologna. The train station, Stazione di Padova, is centrally located, making it easy to reach your accommodation from there.

Driving to Padua is another option, especially if you're planning to explore the surrounding Veneto region. The city is well-connected by highways, and there are several parking options, including public garages and street parking. Just keep in mind that driving in the city center can be challenging due to narrow streets and limited parking spaces.

Getting Around Padua

Once you've arrived in Padua, you'll find that getting around the city is quite straightforward. The historic center is compact and best explored on foot. Walking allows you to fully appreciate the city's charming streets, hidden courtyards, and architectural details.

For longer distances or if you prefer not to walk, Padua has an efficient public transportation system that includes buses and trams. The tram line, known as Linea 1, runs from the northern part of the city to the southern suburbs, passing through key points like the train station, Prato della Valle, and the University of Padua. The trams are modern, clean, and reliable.

Buses are another convenient option, covering areas not served by the tram. You can purchase tickets at kiosks, newsstands, or directly from the bus driver (though it's slightly more expensive on the bus). I recommend getting a day pass or a multi-day pass if you plan on using public transport frequently.

Biking is also popular in Padua, thanks to its flat terrain and bike-friendly streets. There are several bike rental shops throughout the city, and you'll find dedicated bike lanes on many roads. Renting a bike is a great way to explore at your own pace and reach places that might be a bit farther out.

Taxis are available but can be pricey compared to other options. You can find taxi stands at key locations like the train station and major squares, or you can book one by phone or through a mobile app. Ride-sharing services like Uber are not widely available in Padua, so taxis are your best bet for private transport.

Travel Tips and Etiquette

When traveling to a new city, it's always helpful to know a few local customs and etiquette tips to ensure a smooth and respectful visit. Here are some of my top tips for Padua:

1. Greetings and Politeness: Italians are known for their warmth and friendliness. When meeting someone, it's customary to greet them with a **"buongiorno"** (good morning) or **"buonasera"** (good evening). A simple "ciao" is also common among friends. Don't forget to say **"grazie"** (thank you) and **"per favore"** (please) – politeness goes a long way.

2. Dress Code: While Padua is fairly relaxed, it's important to dress appropriately, especially when visiting religious sites like the Basilica of Saint Anthony. Avoid wearing shorts, sleeveless tops, or revealing clothing. A scarf or shawl can be handy to cover your shoulders if needed.

3. Dining Etiquette: Dining in Italy is an experience to be savored. Meals are often leisurely affairs, and it's common to spend several hours enjoying dinner. When eating out, wait for the host or server to seat you. It's customary to order multiple courses, starting with antipasti (appetizers), followed by primi (first course), secondi (second course), and dolci (dessert). Tipping is appreciated but not obligatory – rounding up the bill or leaving a small amount (5-10%) is sufficient.

4. Punctuality: While Italians are known for their relaxed approach to time, it's still important to be punctual for appointments, tours, and reservations. Arriving a few minutes early is considered polite.

5. Respect for Local Customs: Be mindful of local customs and traditions. For example, it's common to take a break in the afternoon (riposo), when many shops and businesses close for a few hours. Use this time to relax, enjoy a leisurely meal, or take a stroll.

6. Language: While many people in Padua speak English, especially in tourist areas, learning a few basic Italian phrases can enhance your experience and show respect for the local culture. Simple phrases like **"dove si trova...?"** (where is...?) and **"quanto costa?"** (how much does it cost?) can be very helpful.

7. Environmental Awareness: Italy places a high value on environmental conservation. Be mindful of your environmental impact by using reusable bags, properly disposing of waste, and conserving water and energy.

8. Safety: Padua is generally a safe city, but it's always wise to take common precautions. Keep an eye on your belongings, especially in crowded areas and on public transport. Avoid walking alone in poorly lit areas at night.

By keeping these tips in mind, you'll be well-prepared to enjoy all that Padua has to offer. Whether you're exploring its historic sites, savoring its culinary delights, or simply soaking in the local atmosphere, your trip to Padua is sure to be an unforgettable adventure.

Chapter 3: Where to Stay

Finding the right place to stay can truly make or break your travel experience, and Padua offers a variety of accommodations to suit every type of traveler. From luxurious hotels to charming bed and breakfasts, the city has something for everyone. During my time in Padua, I had the chance to explore several types of accommodations, and I'm excited to share my insights with you.

Luxury Hotels

For those seeking a taste of luxury, Padua boasts several high-end hotels that offer impeccable service, plush accommodations, and top-notch amenities. Staying in a luxury hotel in Padua means you can enjoy not just comfort and style but also a prime location that puts you close to the city's main attractions.

1. Hotel Majestic Toscanelli

Located in the heart of Padua's historic center, Hotel Majestic Toscanelli is a boutique luxury hotel that exudes elegance and charm. The rooms are beautifully decorated, blending classic Italian style with modern amenities. The hotel offers personalized service, ensuring that every guest feels pampered.

- **Address:** Via dell'Arco, 2, 35122 Padova PD, Italy

- **Phone:** +39 049 663244

- **Website:** www.hotelmajestic.it

2. NH Padova

NH Padova combines modern design with luxurious comfort. Situated near the city center, this hotel offers spacious rooms with contemporary decor, a fitness center, and a rooftop restaurant with stunning views of the city. It's perfect for both business and leisure travelers looking for upscale accommodations.

- **Address:** Via Niccolò Tommaseo, 61, 35131 Padova PD,

Italy

- **Phone:** +39 049 8494111

- **Website:** www.nh-hotels.com

3. Hotel Methis

Nestled along the banks of the River Bacchiglione, Hotel Methis offers a serene retreat with a focus on wellness and relaxation. The hotel's elegant rooms are inspired by the elements of nature, providing a tranquil and rejuvenating atmosphere. The on-site spa and wellness center are perfect for unwinding after a day of exploring.

- **Address:** Riviera Paleocapa, 70, 35141 Padova PD, Italy

- **Phone:** +39 049 8725555

- **Website:** www.hotelmethis.it

Mid-Range Hotels

If you're looking for comfort and convenience without breaking the bank, Padua has a great selection of mid-range hotels. These accommodations offer a good balance of quality and affordability, with many located close to the city's main attractions.

1. Best Western Plus Hotel Galileo

This modern hotel offers a range of amenities, including a fitness center, indoor pool, and on-site restaurant. The rooms are spacious and well-equipped, making it an excellent choice for both business and leisure travelers. Its location near the train station and city center makes it a convenient base for exploring Padua.

- **Address:** Via Venezia, 30, 35131 Padova PD, Italy

- **Phone:** +39 049 7702222

- **Website:** www.bestwestern.it

2. Hotel Al Santo

Just a short walk from the Basilica of Saint Anthony, Hotel Al Santo offers comfortable rooms and a friendly atmosphere. The hotel's central location is perfect for sightseeing, and the staff are always ready to provide tips and recommendations to enhance your stay.

- **Address:** Via del Santo, 147, 35123 Padova PD, Italy

- **Phone:** +39 049 8752131

- **Website:** www.hotelalsanto.it

3. Hotel M14

Located near Prato della Valle, Hotel M14 offers modern accommodations with a touch of elegance. The rooms are stylishly decorated and come with all the necessary amenities. The hotel also provides bike rentals, making it easy to explore the city at your own pace.

- **Address:** Via Acquette, 9, 35122 Padova PD, Italy

- **Phone:** +39 049 8762011

- **Website:** www.hotelm14.it

Budget Accommodations

Traveling on a budget doesn't mean you have to sacrifice comfort or convenience. Padua has several budget-friendly options that offer clean, comfortable accommodations at affordable prices.

1. Hotel Casa del Pellegrino

This budget-friendly hotel is located just steps away from the Basilica of Saint Anthony. It offers basic but comfortable rooms and a warm, welcoming atmosphere. The hotel's central location makes it easy to explore the city without spending a fortune.

- **Address:** Via Melchiorre Cesarotti, 21, 35123 Padova PD, Italy

- **Phone:** +39 049 8239711

- **Website:** www.casadelpellegrino.com

2. Albergo Verdi

Albergo Verdi is a charming budget hotel located in the heart of Padua. The rooms are simple yet cozy, and the staff are friendly and helpful. It's a great option for travelers looking for an affordable place to stay without compromising on location.

- **Address:** Via Dondi dall'Orologio, 7, 35139 Padova PD, Italy

- **Phone:** +39 049 8750822

- **Website:** www.albergoverdipadova.com

3. Hotel Donatello

Situated near the Basilica of Saint Anthony, Hotel Donatello offers budget-friendly accommodations with a focus on comfort and convenience. The rooms are well-maintained, and the hotel provides a range of services to ensure a pleasant stay.

- **Address:** Via del Santo, 102, 35123 Padova PD, Italy

- **Phone:** +39 049 8750634

- **Website:** www.hoteldonatello.net

Unique Stays: B&Bs and Boutique Hotels

For a more personalized and intimate experience, consider staying at one of Padua's charming bed and breakfasts or boutique hotels. These accommodations offer a unique blend of comfort, character, and local flavor.

1. Casa Camilla

This delightful B&B is located in a quiet residential area, offering a peaceful retreat just a short distance from the city center. The rooms are beautifully decorated, and the hosts go above and beyond to make you feel at home. Breakfast is a highlight, featuring homemade treats and local specialties.

- **Address:** Via Pirano, 2, 35135 Padova PD, Italy

- **Phone:** +39 348 2254767

- **Website:** www.bbcasacamilla.com

2. Le Camp Suite & Spa

Le Camp Suite & Spa is a luxurious boutique hotel located in the heart of Padua. The suites are elegantly designed, combining modern amenities with classic Italian style. The on-site spa offers a range of treatments, making it the perfect place to relax and unwind.

- **Address:** Via Giovanni Anghinoni, 10, 35121 Padova PD, Italy

- **Phone:** +39 049 8781234

- **Website:** www.lecampspa.com

3. Scrovegni Room & Breakfast

This charming B&B is located near the Scrovegni Chapel, offering easy access to one of Padua's most famous attractions. The rooms are cozy and well-appointed, and the breakfast is delicious, featuring a variety of fresh, local products.

- **Address:** Via Enrico degli Scrovegni, 7, 35131 Padova PD, Italy

- **Phone:** +39 049 8753406

- **Website:** www.scrovegniroomandbreakfast.it

Family-Friendly Accommodations

Traveling with family requires accommodations that are comfortable, convenient, and cater to the needs of all ages. Padua offers several family-friendly options that ensure a pleasant stay for everyone.

1. Crowne Plaza Padova

Crowne Plaza Padova is a great choice for families, offering spacious rooms and a range of amenities, including a fitness center, restaurant, and kids' play area. The hotel's location near the highway makes it easy to explore Padua and the surrounding region by car.

- **Address:** Via Po, 197, 35135 Padova PD, Italy

- **Phone:** +39 049 8656511

- **Website:** www.ihg.com

2. Hotel Milano

Hotel Milano offers comfortable and family-friendly

accommodations just a short walk from Padua's city center. The rooms are spacious, and the hotel provides amenities such as a restaurant, bar, and free Wi-Fi. The staff are friendly and always ready to assist with any needs.

- **Address:** Via Bronzetti, 62, 35138 Padova PD, Italy

- **Phone:** +39 049 8712555

- **Website:** www.hotelmilano-padova.com

3. Hotel Maritan

Located near the University of Padua, Hotel Maritan is a family-friendly hotel offering comfortable rooms and a range of amenities, including a wellness center. The hotel's central location makes it a convenient base for exploring the city's attractions.

- **Address:** Via Gattamelata, 34, 35128 Padova PD, Italy

- **Phone:** +39 049 685386

- **Website:** www.hotelmaritan.it

Padua offers a wide range of accommodations to suit every

traveler's needs and preferences. Whether you're looking for luxury, comfort, affordability, or a unique stay, you'll find plenty of options that will make your visit to this beautiful city unforgettable.

Chapter 4: Top Tourist Attractions

Padua is a treasure trove of history, culture, and beauty, and exploring its top attractions was an unforgettable experience. As I wandered through the city's ancient streets, I felt like I was stepping back in time, discovering secrets hidden within its historic walls. Here are some of the must-visit attractions that made my time in Padua truly special.

Basilica of Saint Anthony

The Basilica of Saint Anthony, known locally as Il Santo, is one of the most important religious sites in Italy and a major pilgrimage destination. The moment I stepped into the basilica's vast piazza, I was struck by its imposing presence and intricate architectural details. The basilica, built in the 13th century, is a stunning blend of Romanesque, Gothic, and Byzantine styles, reflecting the many centuries of devotion and craftsmanship that went into its creation.

Inside, the basilica is even more breathtaking. The soaring ceilings, adorned with frescoes, create an atmosphere of reverence and awe. The Chapel of the Relics houses the tomb of Saint Anthony, and many visitors come to pay their respects and seek blessings. I was particularly moved by the relics on display, which include Saint Anthony's tongue, jaw, and vocal cords, preserved for centuries.

Don't miss the chance to explore the beautiful cloisters and gardens surrounding the basilica. These serene spaces offer a moment of peace and reflection, away from the bustling city.

- **Address:** Piazza del Santo, 11, 35123 Padova PD, Italy

Scrovegni Chapel

The Scrovegni Chapel, or Cappella degli Scrovegni, is a true gem of Padua, renowned for its stunning frescoes by the master artist Giotto. Visiting this chapel was like stepping into a vivid storybook of medieval life and religious devotion.

The frescoes, painted in the early 14th century, cover the entire interior and depict scenes from the life of the Virgin Mary and Christ, as well as the Last Judgment.

I was captivated by the vivid colors and the expressive detail in each scene. Giotto's work is considered a precursor to the Renaissance, and standing in the chapel, I could see why. The depth and emotion captured in the frescoes are truly remarkable. The highlight for me was the depiction of the Last Judgment, which occupies an entire wall and is both awe-inspiring and humbling.

To preserve the delicate frescoes, visits to the chapel are limited and must be booked in advance. I recommend planning your visit early to ensure you don't miss this extraordinary experience.

- **Address:** Piazza Eremitani, 8, 35121 Padova PD, Italy

Prato della Valle

Prato della Valle is one of the largest squares in Europe, and it's a vibrant hub of activity in Padua. This expansive elliptical square is surrounded by a moat and adorned with 78 statues of notable historical figures, creating a picturesque and inviting atmosphere. On sunny days, locals and tourists alike gather here to relax, stroll, and enjoy the beautiful surroundings.

One of my favorite activities in Prato della Valle was simply people-watching. The square is a melting pot of life, with families, students, and tourists all coming together. The central island, known as Isola Memmia, is a lovely spot for a picnic or a leisurely walk among the trees and flowers.

Every Saturday, the square transforms into a bustling market, where you can find everything from fresh produce and local delicacies to antiques and crafts. It's a fantastic way to experience the local culture and pick up some unique souvenirs.

- **Address:** Prato della Valle, 35121 Padova PD, Italy

Palazzo della Ragione

The Palazzo della Ragione, or Palace of Reason, is a historic civic building that dominates Padua's central square, Piazza delle Erbe. Built in the 13th century, this magnificent palace was once the seat of the city's courts and government. Today, it stands as a testament to Padua's rich history and architectural prowess.

The highlight of the Palazzo della Ragione is its grand hall, known as Il Salone. This vast, open space is one of the largest medieval halls in Europe and is adorned with an impressive fresco cycle that covers the walls and ceiling. The frescoes, depicting astrological themes and scenes from daily life, are a feast for the eyes and provide a fascinating glimpse into medieval thought and culture.

I also enjoyed exploring the ground floor of the palace, which houses a bustling market selling fresh produce, meats, cheeses, and other local goods. It's a lively and colorful scene, and a great place to sample some of Padua's culinary delights.

- **Address:** Piazza delle Erbe, 35122 Padova PD, Italy

Botanical Garden of Padua

The Botanical Garden of Padua, or Orto Botanico di Padova, is the oldest university botanical garden in the world, established in 1545. As a lover of nature and history, I found this garden to be a peaceful and inspiring retreat from the urban hustle and bustle.

The garden is home to an incredible variety of plants from all over the world, arranged in beautifully maintained beds and greenhouses. As I wandered through the garden, I marveled at the exotic plants and ancient trees, some of which have been growing here for centuries. The garden's design reflects the Renaissance ideal of harmony between nature and science, and it's easy to see why it has been designated a UNESCO World Heritage site.

One of the highlights for me was the medicinal plant section, which showcases plants that have been used in traditional medicine for centuries. The garden also features a stunning collection of orchids, cacti, and other rare plants, making it a paradise for botany enthusiasts.

- **Address:** Via Orto Botanico, 15, 35123 Padova PD, Italy

Piazza dei Signori

Piazza dei Signori is one of Padua's most picturesque squares, and spending time here was like stepping into a living postcard. This elegant square, surrounded by beautiful Renaissance buildings, has been a central meeting place for centuries. The square is dominated by the imposing Clock

Tower (Torre dell'Orologio), which features an astronomical clock dating back to the 14th century.

The piazza is always bustling with life, whether it's the lively markets, street performers, or locals enjoying a leisurely coffee at one of the many outdoor cafes. I loved sitting at a cafe, sipping an espresso, and soaking in the vibrant atmosphere. In the evenings, the square is beautifully illuminated, making it a perfect spot for a romantic stroll.

- **Address:** Piazza dei Signori, 35139 Padova PD, Italy

Padua Cathedral

Padua Cathedral, also known as the Cathedral of Santa Maria Assunta, is a significant religious and architectural landmark. The cathedral, with its understated exterior, might not immediately catch your eye, but stepping inside reveals a serene and sacred space. The current structure dates back to the 16th century and was designed by the renowned architect

Andrea Palladio.

The interior of the cathedral is spacious and filled with light, creating a peaceful ambiance. I was particularly struck by the beautiful artwork and the impressive altar. Adjacent to the cathedral is the Baptistery of San Giovanni, which houses stunning frescoes by Giusto de' Menabuoi, depicting scenes from the Bible in vivid detail.

Exploring the cathedral and the baptistery was a deeply moving experience, offering a glimpse into Padua's spiritual heritage and artistic excellence.

- **Address:** Piazza Duomo, 12, 35141 Padova PD, Italy

University of Padua and the Anatomical Theatre

The University of Padua is one of the oldest and most prestigious universities in Europe, founded in 1222. Walking through its historic halls, I felt a sense of awe and inspiration, knowing that this institution has been a center of learning and innovation for centuries. The university has a rich academic heritage, with notable alumni including Galileo Galilei.

One of the highlights of my visit was the Anatomical Theatre, the oldest surviving anatomical theatre in the world. Built in 1594, this unique structure was used for teaching anatomy through public dissections. The tiered seating and the central dissection table create an intimate and fascinating setting, providing a glimpse into the history of medical education.

The university also houses a museum that showcases its scientific and cultural contributions, with exhibits ranging from ancient manuscripts to modern scientific instruments.

- **Address:** Via VIII Febbraio, 2, 35122 Padova PD, Italy

Musei Civici agli Eremitani

The Musei Civici agli Eremitani, or the Civic Museums of the Eremitani, are a must-visit for art and history enthusiasts. This complex of museums is housed in the former Eremitani Monastery and includes the Museum of Archaeology and the Museum of Medieval and Modern Art.

The Museum of Archaeology features an extensive collection of artifacts from ancient civilizations, including Roman, Etruscan, and Greek relics. I was particularly fascinated by the well-preserved mosaics and sculptures that offer insights into the daily life and culture of ancient times.

The Museum of Medieval and Modern Art showcases a remarkable collection of paintings, sculptures, and decorative arts. Highlights include works by Venetian masters such as Tiepolo and Tintoretto. The museum also has a beautiful collection of medieval manuscripts and illuminated texts, which are a testament to the region's rich artistic heritage.

- **Address:** Piazza Eremitani, 8, 35121 Padova PD, Italy

Orto Botanico di Padova

The Orto Botanico di Padova, or the Botanical Garden of Padua, is a haven of tranquility and natural beauty. Established in 1545, it is the oldest university botanical garden in the world and a UNESCO World Heritage site. The garden is a testament to the Renaissance ideal of the harmony between nature and science.

As I strolled through the garden, I was amazed by the diversity of plants, many of which are arranged in thematic sections. The medicinal plant garden was particularly intriguing, with detailed information about the historical and modern uses of various plants. The greenhouses house exotic species from different climates, creating a lush and vibrant environment.

One of the most impressive features of the garden is the ancient plane tree, planted in 1680, which stands as a living monument to the garden's long history. The garden also offers educational exhibits and workshops, making it a wonderful place to learn about botany and ecology.

- **Address:** Via Orto Botanico, 15, 35123 Padova PD, Italy

Exploring these top tourist attractions in Padua was a journey through time, culture, and natural beauty. Each site offers a unique glimpse into the city's rich heritage and vibrant present. From the spiritual and artistic wonders of the Basilica of Saint Anthony and the Scrovegni Chapel to the lively ambiance of Prato della Valle and Piazza dei Signori, Padua is a city that captivates and inspires. Whether you're wandering through the historic halls of the University of Padua or finding peace in the serene Botanical Garden, there's something in Padua for everyone to discover and cherish.

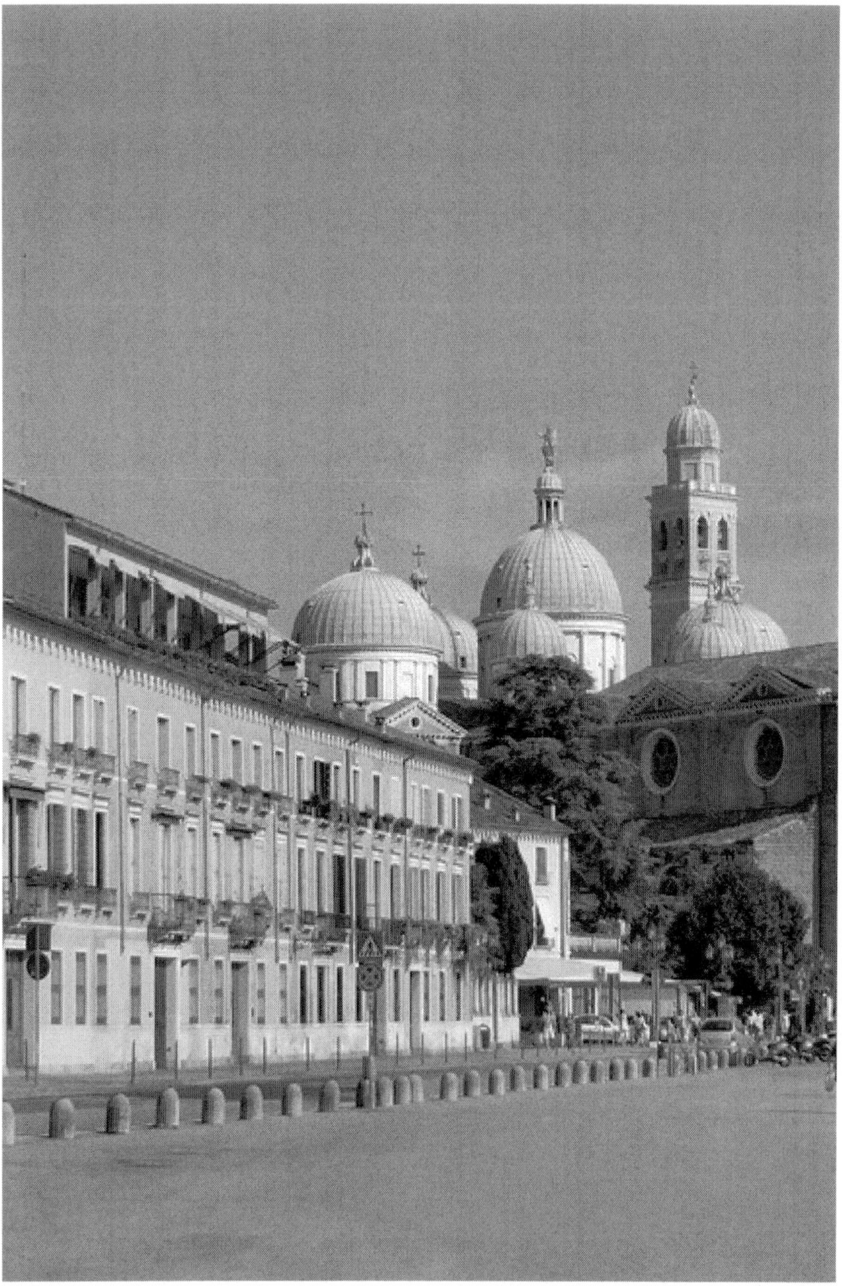

Chapter 5: Exploring Padua's Neighborhoods

Padua is a city that unfolds its charm one neighborhood at a time. Each area has its own unique character, history, and vibe, making it a delight to explore. As I wandered through Padua, I discovered the nuances and hidden gems of its various neighborhoods. Let me take you through some of the most fascinating parts of this captivating city.

Historic City Center

The Historic City Center of Padua is where the heart of the city beats the strongest. Walking through these ancient streets, I felt the weight of history around every corner. The city center is home to some of Padua's most iconic landmarks, bustling piazzas, and charming cafes.

One of the first places I visited was Piazza delle Erbe, a lively square that has been the commercial hub of the city since medieval times. Surrounded by historic buildings and filled with market stalls selling everything from fresh produce to local crafts, the piazza is a sensory delight. Just a stone's throw away is Piazza della Frutta, another bustling market square where I enjoyed mingling with locals and tasting delicious street food.

In the Historic City Center, you'll also find the Palazzo della Ragione, with its stunning frescoed hall and vibrant market on the ground floor. Nearby, the elegant Piazza dei Signori offers a more tranquil atmosphere, perfect for a leisurely coffee break while admiring the Clock Tower.

The cobblestone streets of the city center are lined with shops, restaurants, and historical sites, making it the perfect place to start your exploration of Padua.

- **Address:** Piazza delle Erbe, 35122 Padova PD, Italy

The University District

The University District is a vibrant and youthful area that pulses with the energy of students and academics. The University of Padua, one of the oldest and most prestigious universities in Europe, is the focal point of this neighborhood. Founded in 1222, the university has been a center of learning and innovation for centuries.

Walking through the university's historic campus, I felt a sense of awe at the intellectual heritage that permeates the area. The university buildings are a blend of medieval, Renaissance, and modern architecture, each telling a story of academic pursuit and discovery. One of the highlights of my visit was the Palazzo del Bo, the historic seat of the university. Here, I toured the Anatomical Theatre, the oldest of its kind, and imagined the pioneering medical students who once studied there.

The University District is also home to numerous cafes, bookstores, and cultural venues. It's a lively area where you can enjoy a cup of coffee while watching the lively debates and discussions that spill out onto the streets. The presence of students from all over the world gives the neighborhood a cosmopolitan feel, making it a dynamic and exciting place to explore.

- **Address:** Via VIII Febbraio, 2, 35122 Padova PD, Italy

Jewish Ghetto

The Jewish Ghetto of Padua is a small but historically rich area that offers a poignant glimpse into the city's past. Established in 1603, the ghetto was home to the city's Jewish community until the restrictions were lifted in the 19th century. Today, the narrow streets and hidden courtyards of the ghetto tell a story of resilience and cultural heritage.

As I wandered through the ghetto, I discovered the Great Synagogue, or Tempio Maggiore, which remains a focal point for the Jewish community in Padua. The synagogue, built in the 16th century, is a beautiful example of Renaissance architecture, with a serene and contemplative interior. Visiting the synagogue was a moving experience, as I learned about the history and traditions of Padua's Jewish community.

The ghetto is also home to a number of small shops, galleries, and cafes, each offering a unique insight into the neighborhood's cultural fabric. I particularly enjoyed visiting the Jewish Museum of Padua, which houses a collection of artifacts and exhibits that chronicle the history of the Jewish community in the city.

- **Address:** Via delle Piazze, 26, 35122 Padova PD, Italy

Portello District

The Portello District is a fascinating blend of history and modernity, known for its picturesque canals and vibrant student life. Located near the University of Padua, the district was once the city's main port, playing a crucial role in trade and commerce. Today, it's a lively neighborhood with a youthful vibe, thanks to the presence of many university students.

One of the highlights of the Portello District is the Porta Portello, an impressive 16th-century gate that once served as the main entrance to the city for travelers arriving by boat. The gate is a striking example of Renaissance architecture and offers a glimpse into the city's past as a bustling port.

Walking along the canal, I enjoyed the picturesque views and the lively atmosphere. The area is dotted with trendy bars, cafes, and restaurants, making it a popular spot for both locals and visitors. In the evenings, the district comes alive with music and laughter as people gather to socialize and enjoy the vibrant nightlife.

The Portello District also has several green spaces, such as the Giardini dell'Arena, where you can relax and take in the scenic surroundings. It's a great place to experience the youthful energy and modern spirit of Padua.

- **Address:** Via Portello, 35131 Padova PD, Italy

Arcella Neighborhood

The Arcella Neighborhood is one of Padua's more residential areas, offering a different perspective on the city. Located north of the historic center, Arcella is a multicultural neighborhood with a diverse population and a lively community spirit. Exploring Arcella gave me a sense of the everyday life of Paduans, away from the more touristy areas.

Arcella is known for its vibrant street art and murals, which add a splash of color and creativity to the neighborhood. As I walked through the streets, I was delighted by the various artistic expressions that adorned the buildings, each telling a unique story.

The neighborhood is also home to several local markets, where you can find fresh produce, local delicacies, and handmade crafts. Visiting these markets was a wonderful way to experience the local culture and interact with the friendly residents.

Arcella's diverse population means that you can find a wide range of international cuisine in the neighborhood. From traditional Italian trattorias to ethnic restaurants serving dishes from around the world, there's something to satisfy every palate.

- **Address:** Via Tiziano Aspetti, 35132 Padova PD, Italy

Around Prato della Valle

Prato della Valle is not only one of the largest squares in Europe but also a vibrant neighborhood with plenty to explore. The area around Prato della Valle is a mix of historical sites, green spaces, and cultural attractions, making it a delightful place to spend time.

One of the main attractions in this neighborhood is the

Basilica of Santa Giustina, an imposing church that dates back to the 6th century. The basilica is a stunning example of Renaissance architecture, with a vast interior that exudes a sense of peace and grandeur. I was particularly moved by the tomb of Saint Luke the Evangelist, which is located within the basilica.

Adjacent to Prato della Valle is the Botanical Garden of Padua, a serene and beautiful oasis that offers a welcome escape from the urban hustle and bustle. As I mentioned earlier, this historic garden is a UNESCO World Heritage site and a must-visit for anyone interested in botany and nature.

The area around Prato della Valle is also home to a number of charming cafes, restaurants, and shops. I enjoyed exploring the side streets and discovering hidden gems, from quaint bookshops to artisanal boutiques. The neighborhood has a relaxed and welcoming atmosphere, making it a perfect place to unwind and soak in the beauty of Padua.

- **Address:** Prato della Valle, 35121 Padova PD, Italy

Exploring Padua's neighborhoods was a journey of discovery

and delight. Each area has its own unique charm and character, offering a rich tapestry of experiences that make the city so special. Whether you're wandering through the historic streets of the city center, soaking in the intellectual atmosphere of the University District, or enjoying the multicultural vibe of Arcella, there's always something new to discover in Padua. The vibrant energy of the Portello District and the serene beauty of the area around Prato della Valle add to the city's diverse appeal, making Padua a destination that captivates and enchants at every turn.

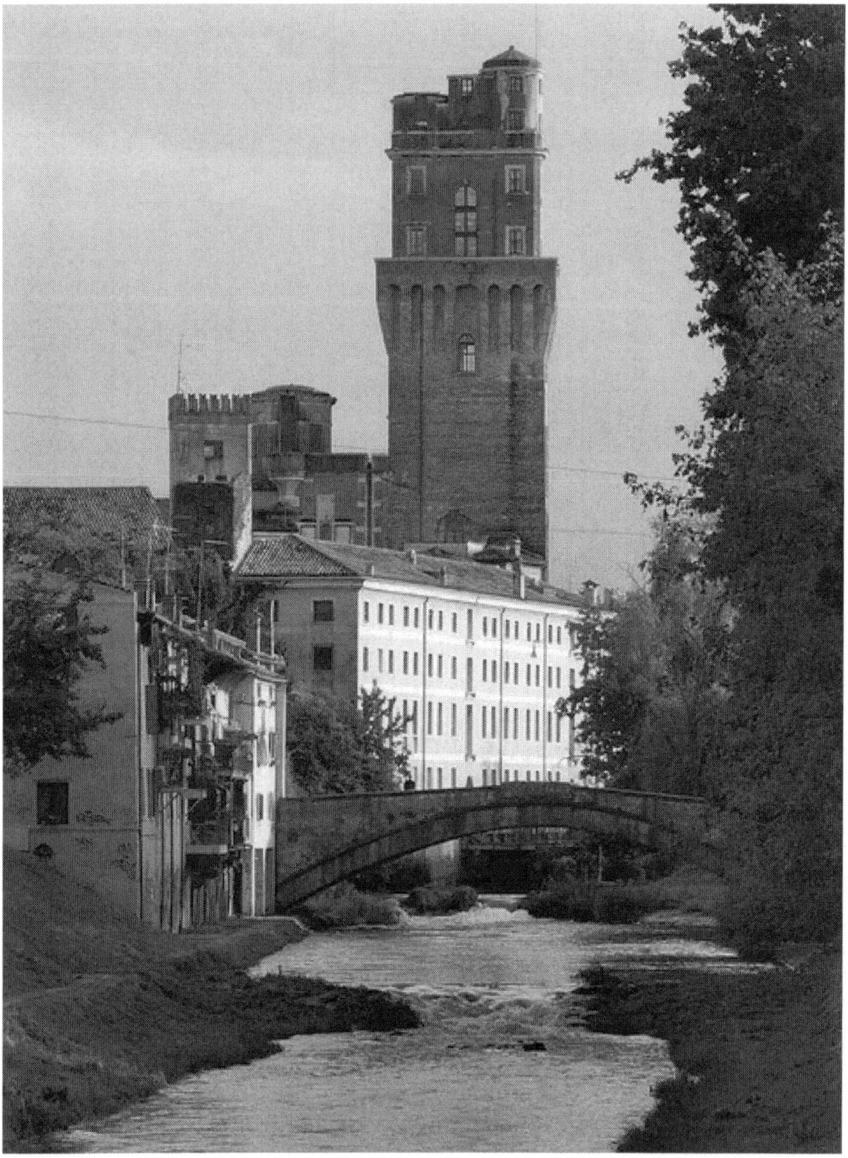

Chapter 6: Dining and Cuisine

Padua is a city that truly comes alive through its flavors. My time here was a culinary adventure, from savoring traditional dishes to discovering hidden gems in cozy cafes. Let me take you on a gastronomic journey through Padua, where every meal tells a story and every bite is a revelation.

Traditional Padua Dishes

One of the best ways to connect with Padua's culture is through its traditional dishes. The cuisine here is a delightful blend of hearty, rustic flavors and refined, elegant dishes that reflect the region's rich culinary heritage.

One dish you absolutely must try is **Bigoli** in Salsa, a type of thick, long pasta served with a savory anchovy and onion sauce. I had this at a charming trattoria called **Trattoria San Pietro** (Via San Pietro, 86, 35139 Padova PD, Italy), and it was an unforgettable experience. The pasta was perfectly cooked, and the sauce had a depth of flavor that was both comforting and complex.

Another traditional favorite is **Risotto al Radicchio**, a creamy risotto made with the slightly bitter red radicchio from the nearby Treviso region. I enjoyed this dish at **Ristorante Belle Parti** (Via Belle Parti, 11, 35139 Padova PD, Italy), where the chef added a touch of balsamic reduction that beautifully balanced the flavors.

For meat lovers, **Bollito Misto** is a must-try. This mixed boiled meat dish is usually served with a variety of sauces, including a zesty salsa verde. **Antica Trattoria dei Paccagnella** (Via del Santo, 113, 35123 Padova PD, Italy) served an exceptional version of this dish, and the cozy, traditional setting made the experience even more special.

And let's not forget dessert. **Pazientina**, a rich, layered cake made with chocolate, custard, and almond paste, is a local favorite. I had the best Pazientina at **Pasticceria Biasetto** (Via Jacopo Facciolati, 12, 35126 Padova PD, Italy), a renowned pastry shop where each bite felt like a celebration.

Best Restaurants for Fine Dining

If you're looking to indulge in a fine dining experience, Padua has plenty to offer. The city boasts several high-end restaurants where you can enjoy exquisite dishes prepared with the finest ingredients.

Le Calandre is one of Padua's most prestigious restaurants, with three Michelin stars to its name. Located just outside the city in **Rubano** (Via Liguria, 1, 35030 Sarmeola di Rubano PD, Italy), it's worth the short trip for a dining experience that borders on the sublime. The tasting menu is a journey through innovative and meticulously crafted dishes, each paired with excellent wines. I still dream about their signature saffron risotto with licorice powder.

In the heart of Padua, **Ristorante La Montecchia** (Via Montecchia, 12, 35030 Selvazzano Dentro PD, Italy) offers a refined dining experience in a beautiful setting. The restaurant is located in a historic villa, and the menu features a modern take on traditional Venetian cuisine. The standout dish for me was the venison fillet with chestnut puree and juniper berries—a perfect blend of rich flavors and elegant presentation.

For a truly unique experience, **Ai Navigli** (Riviera Tiso da Camposampiero, 35010 Padova PD, Italy) offers a menu that focuses on seasonal and locally sourced ingredients. The restaurant's riverside location adds to the charm, and the beautifully plated dishes are a feast for both the eyes and the palate. The black cod with fennel and orange was a revelation, showcasing the chef's skill in balancing flavors.

Casual and Budget Eats

Padua also has a vibrant scene for casual and budget-friendly dining. Whether you're looking for a quick bite or a relaxed meal, there are plenty of options that won't break the bank.

Pizzeria Orsucci (Via Trieste, 11, 35131 Padova PD, Italy) is a fantastic spot for delicious and affordable pizza. The cozy, no-frills atmosphere makes it a popular choice among locals. I tried their Margherita pizza, and the combination of the crispy crust, tangy tomato sauce, and fresh mozzarella was perfection.

For a taste of authentic Italian sandwiches, **Bar dei Osei** (Piazza della Frutta, 13, 35122 Padova PD, Italy) is a great place to stop. Their panini are packed with fresh ingredients and bursting with flavor. I particularly enjoyed the prosciutto and mozzarella panini, which was the perfect midday snack as I explored the city.

Osteria di Fuori Porta (Via Tiziano Aspetti, 7, 35132 Padova PD, Italy) offers a menu of traditional dishes in a relaxed, welcoming environment. The prices are reasonable, and the portions are generous. I had the tagliatelle with wild boar ragu, and it was hearty and satisfying, with rich, meaty flavors that lingered on the palate.

Street Food and Local Markets

Street food and local markets are where you can truly immerse yourself in the local culture and flavors. One of my favorite places to explore was the **Piazza delle Erbe Market** (Piazza delle Erbe, 35122 Padova PD, Italy), where vendors sell everything from fresh produce to artisanal cheeses and cured meats. The bustling atmosphere and the vibrant colors of the stalls made it a sensory delight.

One street food item you must try is Frittelle, sweet fried dough balls often filled with cream or chocolate. I found a fantastic stall near the market that served hot, freshly made frittelle. They were crispy on the outside and soft on the inside, with a sweet, gooey filling that was absolutely addictive.

For a more substantial street food experience, Tigelleria Tigellino (Via Umberto I, 64, 35122 Padova PD, Italy) offers a variety of tigelle, a type of small, round bread typically filled with cured meats, cheeses, and spreads. I tried one filled with prosciutto, stracchino cheese, and arugula, and it was the perfect blend of savory and creamy.

Cafes and Gelaterias

Padua's cafe culture is vibrant and inviting, offering a perfect spot to relax and people-watch. One of my favorite cafes was **Caffè Pedrocchi** (Via VIII Febbraio, 15, 35122 Padova PD, Italy), a historic establishment known as the **"cafe without doors"** because it was once open 24/7. The elegant interior and the rich history make it a must-visit. I enjoyed a classic espresso paired with a delicious pastry called Pedrocchino, a custard-filled delight.

When it comes to gelato, Padua has some outstanding

options. **Gelateria Giotto** (Via Eremitani, 1, 35121 Padova PD, Italy) is renowned for its high-quality, artisanal gelato. The flavors are rich and intense, made with natural ingredients. I tried the pistachio and dark chocolate, and both were incredibly creamy and flavorful.

Another great spot is **Gelateria La Romana** (Via G. Matteotti, 10, 35137 Padova PD, Italy), where the gelato is made fresh daily. The variety of flavors is impressive, and the staff is happy to let you sample before making your choice. My favorite was the salted caramel, which had the perfect balance of sweet and salty.

Vegetarian and Vegan Options

Padua is also welcoming to vegetarians and vegans, with a growing number of restaurants catering to plant-based diets. **Radicchio Rosso** (Via del Santo, 42, 35123 Padova PD, Italy) offers a menu full of creative and flavorful vegetarian dishes. I had the pumpkin risotto, which was creamy and rich, with the natural sweetness of the pumpkin shining through.

For a fully vegan experience, **Biogusto** (Via Roma, 63, 35122 Padova PD, Italy) is a fantastic choice. The menu features a variety of vegan dishes made with organic ingredients. I tried the vegan lasagna, which was hearty and satisfying, with layers of rich tomato sauce, vegetables, and a delicious vegan béchamel.

Another great option is **L'Angolo Verde** (Via Sorio, 35, 35141 Padova PD, Italy), which offers a range of vegetarian and vegan dishes in a cozy, welcoming setting. The tofu stir-fry with seasonal vegetables was a standout, bursting with fresh flavors and perfectly cooked.

Dining in Padua was an adventure in itself, each meal an opportunity to connect with the city's rich culinary heritage and vibrant contemporary food scene. From the traditional dishes that tell the story of the region to the innovative creations of its fine dining restaurants, every bite was a testament to the passion and creativity of Padua's chefs.

The casual eateries and street food stalls offered a more relaxed but equally delicious experience, while the cafes and gelaterias provided the perfect spots to indulge in sweet treats and soak in the city's atmosphere. And with plenty of options for vegetarians and vegans, Padua truly has something for everyone. Whether you're a food enthusiast or just looking for a good meal, Padua's dining scene is sure to leave you satisfied and eager for more.

Chapter 7: Shopping in Padua

When I traveled to Padua, I found that shopping was not just about picking up souvenirs—it was about immersing myself in the local culture, discovering unique items, and enjoying the city's vibrant atmosphere. From bustling markets to charming artisan shops, and from fashionable boutiques to large shopping centers, Padua offers a diverse shopping experience that caters to every taste and budget. Let me take you through the best spots in town where I indulged my shopping cravings.

Markets and Bazaars

Markets in Padua are a treasure trove of local goods, fresh produce, and unique finds. One of the first markets I visited was the **Piazza delle Erbe Market** (Piazza delle Erbe, 35122 Padova PD, Italy). This bustling market has been a central part of Padua's commerce for centuries. As I wandered through the stalls, I was greeted by a colorful array of fruits, vegetables, cheeses, and cured meats. The atmosphere was lively, with vendors enthusiastically showcasing their products and locals chatting as they picked out their groceries.

Another must-visit market is the **Piazza della Frutta Market** (Piazza della Frutta, 35122 Padova PD, Italy), which runs parallel to the Piazza delle Erbe. It's a great place to find fresh flowers, artisan bread, and local specialties. I found the variety of cheeses particularly impressive and couldn't resist picking up some local pecorino to take home.

For a more eclectic shopping experience, the **Antique Market at Piazza dei Signori** (Piazza dei Signori, 35139 Padova PD, Italy) is a fantastic spot. Held on the second Sunday of each month, this market features antiques, vintage items, and unique collectibles. I spent hours browsing through old books, vintage jewelry, and antique furniture, and I even managed to pick up a beautiful old map of Padua as a memento.

Local Artisan Shops

Exploring Padua's artisan shops was one of my favorite experiences. These small, often family-run businesses offer handcrafted goods that reflect the city's rich tradition of craftsmanship.

Ceramiche Mazzotti (Via Giotto, 8, 35121 Padova PD, Italy) is a charming shop known for its high-quality ceramics. The collection includes beautifully designed plates, bowls, and vases, all handcrafted with intricate patterns. I bought a set of hand-painted espresso cups that now have a special place in my kitchen.

If you're looking for artisanal leather goods, **Pelletteria Fiorentina** (Via Umberto I, 47, 35122 Padova PD, Italy) is a must-visit. This shop offers a wide range of leather products, from elegant handbags to classic wallets. The quality of the leather is exceptional, and the craftsmanship is evident in every piece. I ended up purchasing a stylish leather belt that has become one of my favorite accessories.

For a unique gift, head to **La Bottega del Tartufo** (Via Roma, 28, 35122 Padova PD, Italy), a shop dedicated to truffle products. They offer a variety of truffle-infused oils, sauces, and even truffle-flavored chocolates. I bought a jar of truffle honey that made for an excellent gift and a delicious addition to my pantry.

Souvenirs and Gifts

Picking up souvenirs in Padua is all about finding something that captures the essence of the city. **Bottega del Vino** (Via dei Fabbri, 4, 35122 Padova PD, Italy) is an excellent place to find local wines and culinary delights. They offer a wide selection of regional wines, including the famous Veneto reds. I picked up a bottle of Amarone to remember my time in Padua, and it made for a fantastic gift as well.

For more traditional souvenirs, **Il Mercato delle Pulci** (Via Sant'Agostino, 11, 35121 Padova PD, Italy) is a delightful flea market with a variety of items. From vintage postcards and antique maps to handmade jewelry and local crafts, it's a great place to find something unique. I found a lovely hand-painted ceramic tile featuring a scene of Padua's historic architecture.

If you're looking for something specifically Paduan, **La Casa**

del Sarto (Via della Frutta, 14, 35122 Padova PD, Italy) offers a selection of local artisanal products, including traditional Venetian masks and handcrafted glass items. I bought a beautiful Venetian mask that now hangs proudly in my home, reminding me of the intricate artistry I encountered in Padua.

Shopping Malls and Outlets

For those who prefer a more modern shopping experience, Padua has several shopping malls and outlets that offer a wide range of international and Italian brands. **Centro Commerciale Giotto** (Via Giotto, 10, 35121 Padova PD, Italy) is a popular mall located near the city center. It features a mix of high-street fashion stores, electronics shops, and a large food court. I enjoyed browsing through the latest fashion trends and picked up a couple of Italian-designed clothing items.

Another excellent shopping destination is **Centro Commerciale Padova Est** (Via Primaticcio, 1, 35132 Padova PD, Italy), a large mall with a variety of stores, including international brands and local boutiques. The mall also has a hypermarket where you can find everything from groceries to home goods. I spent a few hours exploring the diverse range of stores and indulging in some retail therapy.

For outlet shopping, **Noventa di Piave Designer Outlet** (Via Marco Polo, 1, 30020 Noventa di Piave VE, Italy) is worth a visit. Located a short drive from Padua, this outlet offers discounted prices on designer brands and luxury goods. I found some fantastic deals on Italian leather accessories and high-end clothing, making it a great place to shop for premium items at reduced prices.

Shopping in Padua was more than just a chance to buy things; it was an opportunity to dive into the city's culture and history. Whether I was haggling at a bustling market, discovering unique artisan crafts, or indulging in some high-end retail therapy, each shopping experience added a new layer to my understanding of Padua.

From the vibrant markets and charming local shops to the modern malls and outlet centers, Padua offers a shopping experience that caters to all tastes and budgets. So, whether you're looking for a special souvenir, a taste of local craftsmanship, or a little bit of luxury, Padua has something to offer every shopper.

Chapter 8: Arts, Culture, and Entertainment

Padua, with its rich history and vibrant cultural scene, truly comes alive through its arts, culture, and entertainment. Whether you're a lover of the theater, a museum enthusiast, or someone who enjoys a lively night out, Padua offers a diverse array of experiences that cater to all interests. My time in this charming city allowed me to delve deep into its cultural offerings, and I'm excited to share my discoveries with you.

Theaters and Concert Halls

Theater and music are deeply ingrained in Padua's cultural fabric. One of the city's standout venues is the **Teatro Verdi**

(Piazza Verdi, 1, 35100 Padova PD, Italy). This historic theater, built in the 18th century, is renowned for its opulent interior and excellent acoustics. I attended a performance of Verdi's La Traviata, and the experience was nothing short of magical. The ornate decor and the passionate performance created an unforgettable evening.

Another gem is the **Teatro Altinate** (Via Altinate, 71, 35121 Padova PD, Italy), a versatile space that hosts a range of performances from classical concerts to contemporary theater. The intimate setting made for an engaging experience, and I was particularly impressed by the acoustics during a chamber music concert I attended. The theater's blend of modern amenities with historic charm is a testament to Padua's dedication to the arts.

For a more contemporary theater experience, **Teatro de' Rossi** (Via del Vescovado, 12, 35121 Padova PD, Italy) offers a range of innovative performances and experimental works. The theater's modern design and diverse programming provide a refreshing contrast to the city's historic venues. I caught a cutting-edge performance art piece that was thought-provoking and engaging, showcasing the city's dynamic arts scene.

Museums and Art Galleries

Padua's museums and art galleries offer a deep dive into its artistic heritage and contemporary creativity. One of the must-visit museums is the **Museo di Padova** (Prato della Valle, 1, 35123 Padova PD, Italy). This museum is a treasure trove of local history, featuring everything from ancient artifacts to Renaissance art. The highlight for me was the extensive collection of medieval sculptures and frescoes, which provided a fascinating glimpse into Padua's artistic evolution.

Just a short walk from the museum is the **Palazzo della Ragione** (Piazza delle Erbe, 35122 Padova PD, Italy). This medieval palace doubles as an art gallery, showcasing works from the 13th to the 19th centuries. The building itself is a masterpiece of medieval architecture, and the art exhibits within are equally impressive. The frescoes on the upper floor, depicting the zodiac signs and historical scenes, are particularly captivating.

For contemporary art, **Galleria Cavour** (Piazza Cavour, 7, 35122 Padova PD, Italy) offers a vibrant space featuring works by both emerging and established artists. The gallery's rotating exhibitions ensure that there's always something new to see. I visited during an exhibition of modern abstract art and was struck by the creativity and depth of the pieces on display.

Another gem is the **Museo Bottacin** (Via del Santo, 11, 35123 Padova PD, Italy), which houses an eclectic collection of artifacts, including ancient coins, manuscripts, and rare books. The museum's exhibits are a testament to Padua's rich intellectual history, and the detailed descriptions provided valuable insights into the artifacts.

Festivals and Events

Padua's festival calendar is packed with events that celebrate everything from local traditions to international cultures. One of the city's most famous events is the **Festa di Sant'Antonio** (June 13, various locations), a festival honoring the city's patron saint. The celebrations include a lively procession through the city, music performances, and food stalls offering local delicacies. Participating in this festival gave me a deeper appreciation for Padua's vibrant community spirit.

Another highlight is the **Padova Jazz Festival** (various locations, usually in October). This annual event attracts jazz musicians from around the world and features a range of performances from classic to contemporary jazz. I attended a fantastic concert at the **Centro Culturale Altinate** (Via Altinate, 71, 35121 Padova PD, Italy), where the intimate setting allowed for an up-close and personal musical experience.

For those interested in literature, the **Padova Book Fair** (usually held in April at the Centro Culturale Altinate) is a must-visit. The fair features book signings, readings, and discussions with authors, providing a platform for both established and emerging writers. I enjoyed exploring the various book stalls and attending a panel discussion on contemporary Italian literature.

Nightlife and Bars

Padua's nightlife is as varied as its cultural offerings. From chic cocktail bars to lively pubs, the city has something for every taste. One of my favorite spots was **Caffè Pedrocchi** (Via VIII Febbraio, 15, 35122 Padova PD, Italy), a historic café that transforms into a lively bar in the evening. The grand interior and extensive cocktail menu made it the perfect place to unwind after a day of sightseeing.

For a more contemporary vibe, **Osteria dei Savi** (Via Mazzini, 7, 35100 Padova PD, Italy) offers a trendy atmosphere with a great selection of craft beers and innovative cocktails. The bar's stylish décor and friendly staff created a relaxed environment where I enjoyed sampling various drinks and tapas.

If you're looking for live music, **Bar Azzurro** (Via della Croce, 5, 35122 Padova PD, Italy) is a popular choice. The bar frequently hosts local bands and musicians, creating a lively and engaging atmosphere. I was treated to an energetic performance by a local rock band, which made for a memorable night out.

Cinema and Performing Arts

Padua has a thriving cinema and performing arts scene that offers a range of options from classic films to avant-garde performances. **Cinema Pio X** (Via San Giovanni, 10, 35121 Padova PD, Italy) is a historic cinema that screens both mainstream and independent films. The vintage charm of the cinema, coupled with its diverse film offerings, made for a delightful movie night.

For those interested in performing arts, **Teatro delle Maddalene** (Via delle Maddalene, 4, 35123 Padova PD, Italy) is a fantastic venue that hosts a variety of performances, including classical music, dance, and theater. I attended a ballet performance here that was beautifully staged and thoroughly enjoyable.

Cinemalta (Via Santa Croce, 2, 35122 Padova PD, Italy) is another excellent choice for film enthusiasts. This independent cinema focuses on international and art-house films, providing a unique alternative to mainstream offerings. The intimate setting and curated selection of films made it a great place to catch something different.

Music and Dance

Music and dance are integral to Padua's cultural life, and the city offers plenty of opportunities to enjoy both. **The Padua Symphony Orchestra** (Piazza dei Signori, 1, 35139 Padova PD, Italy) performs regularly at various venues throughout the city, including the Teatro Verdi. I attended a symphony concert that showcased a range of classical compositions, and the quality of the performance was exceptional.

For dance enthusiasts, **Centro Studi Danza** (Via Cavour, 16, 35100 Padova PD, Italy) offers a range of dance classes and performances. The center hosts regular shows that feature both classical and contemporary dance, and attending one of their performances was a highlight of my visit.

Club Jazz (Via dei Mercanti, 5, 35122 Padova PD, Italy) is a popular venue for live jazz performances and dance events. The club's lively atmosphere and excellent acoustics make it a great place to enjoy a night of music and dancing. I had a fantastic time dancing to a live jazz band and soaking up the energetic vibe of the venue.

Exploring Padua's arts, culture, and entertainment scene was a deeply enriching experience. From the historic theaters and modern galleries to the lively festivals and vibrant nightlife, Padua offers a wealth of opportunities to immerse oneself in its cultural life.

Each venue and event added a new dimension to my understanding of the city, making my time there both memorable and inspiring. Whether you're a culture buff, a music lover, or someone who enjoys a good night out, Padua has something to offer that will leave you captivated and eager to return.

Chapter 9: Outdoor Activities and Nature

Padua isn't just a city of historic architecture and vibrant culture—it's also a fantastic destination for outdoor enthusiasts and nature lovers. During my time there, I discovered that the city offers an impressive range of activities that allow you to enjoy its green spaces, explore its surroundings, and immerse yourself in nature. Whether you're a casual stroller or an adventurous explorer, Padua has something to offer. Let me take you through some of the best outdoor activities and natural experiences I had while visiting this charming Italian city.

Parks and Gardens

One of my favorite ways to unwind in Padua was to explore its beautiful parks and gardens. **Prato della Valle** (Piazza Prato della Valle, 35123 Padova PD, Italy) is a sprawling square that's also the largest public square in Italy. It's surrounded by a canal and is dotted with statues of prominent historical figures. Strolling around this picturesque space, I was mesmerized by the lush greenery and the serene ambiance. The park is ideal for a leisurely walk or a picnic, and it's a popular spot for locals and tourists alike to relax and enjoy the outdoors.

Another gem is the **Botanical Garden of Padua** (Orto Botanico, Via dell'Orto Botanico, 15, 35123 Padova PD, Italy), which is one of the oldest botanical gardens in the world. Founded in 1545, the garden is a UNESCO World Heritage site and offers a diverse collection of plants from around the globe. Wandering through the beautifully curated sections, including the tropical greenhouse and the medicinal plant garden, provided a peaceful escape from the city's hustle and bustle. The garden's historical significance and natural beauty made it a highlight of my trip.

For a more local experience, I visited **Parco Montirone** (Via Montirone, 35129 Padova PD, Italy), a smaller but charming park on the outskirts of the city. It's less crowded than the more famous parks and offers a tranquil setting with walking paths and playgrounds. It's a great place to experience Padua's natural side without the hustle of tourist spots.

Walking and Cycling Tours

Exploring Padua on foot or by bike is a wonderful way to see the city from a different perspective. I opted for a walking tour that took me through some of the city's most historic and scenic areas. One of the most enjoyable routes was the Ancient City Walls Walk, which follows the remnants of Padua's medieval walls. Starting at the **Porta Savonarola** (Piazza Savonarola, 35122 Padova PD, Italy), the tour led me along the old city fortifications, offering views of historic gates and bastions. The walk was both informative and scenic, providing insights into Padua's rich history while showcasing some lovely urban green spaces.

For cycling enthusiasts, Padua offers several cycling tours that explore the city and its surroundings. I took a guided tour with **Bike Experience Padova** (Via Umberto I, 40, 35122 Padova PD, Italy), which provided a fantastic way to see the city's highlights while getting some exercise. The tour took us through picturesque streets, past historic landmarks, and along scenic paths. One of the standout segments was the ride along the River Bacchiglione, which offered a peaceful and scenic route away from the city center.

The city is also connected to a network of cycling trails that lead out into the surrounding countryside. One notable trail is the Padua to Venice Cycle Path, which follows the River Brenta and offers stunning views of the Italian countryside. I didn't have time to complete the full trail, but even a short ride provided a refreshing change of scenery and a glimpse into the beautiful landscape beyond the city.

Day Trips and Excursions

Padua's location in northern Italy makes it an ideal base for exploring nearby attractions. One of the most memorable day trips I took was to **Villa dei Vescovi** (Via dei Vescovi, 1, 35030 Luvigliano PD, Italy), a stunning Renaissance villa located about 30 minutes from Padua. The villa is set amidst rolling hills and offers guided tours of its beautifully preserved rooms and gardens. The views from the villa's terrace were absolutely breathtaking, and the peaceful surroundings made for a perfect escape from the city.

Another fantastic excursion was to the **Colli Euganei Regional Park** (Via Ca' Mureda, 1, 35037 Teolo PD, Italy), located just a short drive from Padua. This park is known for its volcanic hills, lush forests, and charming villages. I spent a day hiking through the park's trails, enjoying the fresh air and beautiful landscapes. The trails vary in difficulty, so there's something for everyone, whether you're looking for a leisurely stroll or a more challenging hike.

If you're interested in exploring more historic sites, a visit to **Montagnana** (Montagnana, 35044 PD, Italy), a medieval town located about an hour from Padua, is highly recommended. The town is renowned for its well-preserved city walls and historic architecture. Wandering through Montagnana's charming streets felt like stepping back in time, and the town's historic ambiance was truly captivating.

Boating on the River Bacchiglione

One of the most relaxing ways to experience Padua's natural beauty is to take a boat ride on the River Bacchiglione. I decided to rent a rowboat from **Navigazione Bacchiglione** (Lungargine Bassi, 35139 Padova PD, Italy) and spend a few hours on the water. The river winds through the city, providing a unique vantage point for viewing Padua's architecture and green spaces. As I floated along, I admired the reflections of the city's historic buildings on the water and enjoyed the peaceful ambiance of the riverbanks.

The boat rental was straightforward, and the staff at Navigazione Bacchiglione provided all the necessary instructions and equipment. Whether you choose to row yourself or take a guided boat tour, spending time on the river is a wonderful way to unwind and appreciate the city's natural surroundings.

Sports and Recreation

For those who enjoy more active pursuits, Padua offers a

range of sports and recreational activities. I was particularly impressed by the city's sports facilities and the variety of options available for both casual and serious athletes.

One of the highlights was the **Padova Sport Center** (Via G. P. Colleoni, 15, 35142 Padova PD, Italy), which features a wide range of facilities including tennis courts, swimming pools, and fitness centers. I took advantage of the outdoor swimming pool, which was a great way to cool off after a day of exploring. The center's modern amenities and well-maintained facilities made it a top choice for anyone looking to stay active while visiting the city.

For golf enthusiasts, **Golf Club Padova** (Via del Golf, 1, 35100 Padova PD, Italy) is located just outside the city and offers a beautiful 18-hole course set amidst lush greenery. The course is well-designed, with challenging holes and scenic views. I spent a relaxing afternoon playing a round of golf and enjoyed the peaceful setting and excellent facilities.

Additionally, **Padua's Central Park** (Parco delle Tre Torri, 35127 Padova PD, Italy) offers various recreational options including jogging paths, sports fields, and picnic areas. It's a great spot to engage in some light sports activities or simply enjoy a leisurely walk or jog in a pleasant environment.

My time in Padua allowed me to explore a range of outdoor activities and natural beauty that truly enhanced my travel experience. From strolling through historic parks and cycling along scenic trails to enjoying peaceful boat rides and engaging in recreational sports, Padua offered a wealth of opportunities to connect with nature and enjoy its stunning landscapes. Whether you're looking for a relaxing day in the park, an adventurous hike, or a unique way to see the city from the water, Padua has something to offer every outdoor enthusiast.

Chapter 10: Itineraries for Every Traveler

Padua is a city rich in history, culture, and natural beauty, making it an ideal destination for a variety of travelers. Whether you're planning a quick weekend escape, a family vacation, or a romantic getaway, there's something for everyone in this charming Italian city. Let me guide you through some detailed itineraries tailored to different interests and types of travelers, based on my own experiences exploring Padua.

Weekend Getaway

Day 1

Morning:

Start your weekend with a leisurely breakfast at Caffè

Pedrocchi (Via VIII Febbraio, 15, 35122 Padova PD, Italy). This historic café offers a delightful selection of pastries and coffee in a beautifully ornate setting. After breakfast, head to Prato della Valle (Piazza Prato della Valle, 35123 Padova PD, Italy), the largest public square in Italy. Take a stroll around the square, admire the statues, and enjoy the picturesque canal that surrounds it.

Afternoon:

Visit the Basilica of Saint Anthony (Piazza del Santo, 35123 Padova PD, Italy), a stunning example of Italian architecture and a significant religious site. Spend some time exploring the basilica and its beautiful interior. For lunch, head to Osteria dei Savi (Via Mazzini, 7, 35100 Padova PD, Italy) for a taste of local cuisine. Afterward, make your way to the Scrovegni Chapel (Cappella degli Scrovegni, Piazza Eremitani, 35121 Padova PD, Italy) to marvel at Giotto's famous frescoes.

Evening:

Enjoy dinner at Ristorante La Finestra (Via della Croce, 6, 35122 Padova PD, Italy), known for its exquisite Italian dishes. After dinner, take a leisurely walk along the River

Bacchiglione, soaking in the city lights and the peaceful ambiance.

Day 2

Morning:

Start your day with a visit to the Botanical Garden of Padua (Orto Botanico, Via dell'Orto Botanico, 15, 35123 Padova PD, Italy). Spend a few hours wandering through the diverse plant collections and relaxing in the serene environment. For brunch, stop by Caffè Pasticceria Zanon (Via San Fermo, 2, 35121 Padova PD, Italy) for some delicious pastries and coffee.

Afternoon:

Explore the Palazzo della Ragione (Piazza delle Erbe, 35122 Padova PD, Italy) and its fascinating medieval architecture. Spend some time shopping in the nearby Piazza delle Erbe market, where you can find local goods and souvenirs. For a mid-afternoon snack, try Gelateria La Romana (Via Umberto I, 8, 35122 Padova PD, Italy), known for its exceptional gelato.

Evening:

Wrap up your weekend with a dinner at Ristorante Da Giovanni (Via P. del Prato, 14, 35123 Padova PD, Italy), offering a range of traditional Italian dishes. If you have energy left, enjoy a drink at Bar Azzurro (Via della Croce, 5, 35122 Padova PD, Italy) and soak in the lively atmosphere.

Family-Friendly Itinerary

Day 1

Morning:

Start with a hearty breakfast at Pasticceria Pinton (Via delle Piazze, 3, 35123 Padova PD, Italy), which offers delicious pastries and family-friendly options. After breakfast, visit the Padua Botanical Garden (Orto Botanico, Via dell'Orto Botanico, 15, 35123 Padova PD, Italy), where kids can explore the different plant species and enjoy the open spaces. The garden is a great place for a family picnic.

Afternoon:

Head to Parco Montirone (Via Montirone, 35129 Padova PD, Italy) for some outdoor fun. The park features playgrounds and plenty of space for kids to run around. For lunch, try

Trattoria da Fabio (Via dei Tadi, 5, 35129 Padova PD, Italy), which offers a family-friendly menu with traditional Italian dishes. After lunch, visit the Museo di Padova (Prato della Valle, 1, 35123 Padova PD, Italy), where interactive exhibits and historical artifacts will engage both children and adults.

Evening:

For dinner, head to Osteria dei Savi (Via Mazzini, 7, 35100 Padova PD, Italy), which is known for its relaxed atmosphere and family-friendly menu. After dinner, take a relaxed stroll along Prato della Valle, where the kids can enjoy the open space and the illuminated fountains.

Day 2

Morning:

Start with breakfast at Caffè del Museo (Piazza Eremitani, 35121 Padova PD, Italy), which offers a selection of pastries and kid-friendly options. Spend the morning at Leolandia (Via Leolandia, 1, 24040 Capriate San Gervasio BG, Italy), an amusement park located a bit outside Padua but worth the trip for a day full of family-friendly rides and attractions.

Afternoon:

Return to Padua for lunch at Ristorante Pizzeria Al Duomo (Piazza Duomo, 1, 35141 Padova PD, Italy), where you can enjoy delicious pizzas and pasta dishes. In the afternoon, visit the Museo degli Eremitani (Piazza Eremitani, 35121 Padova PD, Italy), which has a range of art and historical exhibits that can capture the interest of both adults and children.

Evening:

For dinner, head to Ristorante Pizzeria La Tana (Via della Provvidenza, 7, 35124 Padova PD, Italy), offering a casual dining experience with a wide selection of pizzas. If time allows, consider a relaxing boat ride on the River Bacchiglione to end the day on a peaceful note.

Romantic Retreat

Day 1

Morning:

Begin your romantic getaway with a breakfast at Caffè Pedrocchi (Via VIII Febbraio, 15, 35122 Padova PD, Italy). The elegant setting and delicious pastries make it a perfect start to a romantic day. Afterward, head to the Basilica of

Saint Anthony (Piazza del Santo, 35123 Padova PD, Italy). Take a moment to explore the serene interior and the surrounding piazza.

Afternoon:

Have a romantic lunch at Ristorante Antico Brolo (Via del Brolo, 1, 35100 Padova PD, Italy), which offers a charming atmosphere and exquisite Italian cuisine. After lunch, take a leisurely stroll through the Botanical Garden of Padua (Orto Botanico, Via dell'Orto Botanico, 15, 35123 Padova PD, Italy). The serene gardens provide a lovely backdrop for a romantic walk.

Evening:

Enjoy a candlelit dinner at Ristorante La Folperia (Piazza delle Erbe, 1, 35122 Padova PD, Italy), known for its intimate ambiance and fine dining. After dinner, take a romantic walk along the River Bacchiglione and enjoy the night views of the city.

Day 2

Morning:

Start your day with a brunch at Caffè della Storia (Via dei

Tadi, 7, 35100 Padova PD, Italy), which offers a cozy setting and delicious brunch options. Then, visit the Scrovegni Chapel (Cappella degli Scrovegni, Piazza Eremitani, 35121 Padova PD, Italy) to admire Giotto's frescoes in a serene and quiet environment.

Afternoon:

For a romantic and relaxing afternoon, take a trip to the Villa dei Vescovi (Via dei Vescovi, 1, 35030 Luvigliano PD, Italy). Explore the beautiful villa and its gardens, which offer stunning views of the surrounding landscape. Enjoy a leisurely lunch at the villa's restaurant or a nearby café.

Evening:

End your romantic retreat with a special dinner at Ristorante Il Desco (Via San Giovanni, 12, 35121 Padova PD, Italy). The elegant setting and exceptional cuisine provide a perfect conclusion to your stay. After dinner, consider a nightcap at Caffè Minerva (Via dei Mercanti, 8, 35122 Padova PD, Italy), where you can enjoy a quiet drink and reflect on your romantic getaway.

Cultural Enthusiast

Day 1

Morning:

Begin your day with a rich breakfast at Caffè della Piazzetta (Piazza dei Signori, 7, 35139 Padova PD, Italy), which offers a taste of local flavor. After breakfast, immerse yourself in history with a visit to the Palazzo della Ragione (Piazza delle Erbe, 35122 Padova PD, Italy). Explore its impressive medieval architecture and fascinating exhibits.

Afternoon:

For lunch, head to Trattoria Al 4 Soldi (Via del Santo, 10, 35123 Padova PD, Italy), which offers traditional dishes in a historical setting. Afterward, visit the Museo degli Eremitani (Piazza Eremitani, 35121 Padova PD, Italy) and the adjacent Scrovegni Chapel (Cappella degli Scrovegni, Piazza Eremitani, 35121 Padova PD, Italy) to explore Padua's rich artistic heritage.

Evening:

Enjoy dinner at Ristorante La Montecchia (Via Montecchia, 10, 35100 Padova PD, Italy), known for its historical ambiance and traditional cuisine. After dinner, attend a performance at the Teatro Verdi (Piazza Giuseppe Verdi, 35100 Padova PD, Italy), a beautiful opera house that hosts a variety of cultural events.

Day 2

Morning:

Start with breakfast at Caffè Pasticceria Zanon (Via San Fermo, 2, 35121 Padova PD, Italy), offering a selection of pastries and coffee. Visit the University of Padua (Via 8 Febbraio, 2, 35122 Padova PD, Italy) and its Anatomical Theatre (Via 8 Febbraio, 2, 35122 Padova PD, Italy), one of the oldest medical theatres in Europe. Explore the university's historical buildings and learn about its significant role in academic history.

Afternoon:

For lunch, try Ristorante Al Bacco (Via delle Rose, 3, 35100 Padova PD, Italy), offering a range of traditional Italian dishes. Spend your afternoon at the Musei Civici agli Eremitani (Piazza Eremitani, 35121 Padova PD, Italy), where you can explore the art and historical collections.

Evening:

Dine at Ristorante Da Giovanni (Via P. del Prato, 14, 35123 Padova PD, Italy), known for its authentic Italian cuisine. For a nightcap, head to Caffè delle Arti (Piazza delle Erbe, 3, 35122 Padova PD, Italy), a charming café with a rich history and a cozy atmosphere.

Outdoor Adventure

Day 1

Morning:

Start your day with breakfast at Caffè Pedrocchi (Via VIII Febbraio, 15, 35122 Padova PD, Italy). Afterward, embark on a cycling tour with Bike Experience Padova (Via Umberto I, 40, 35122 Padova PD, Italy). Explore the city's bike paths and scenic routes, including a ride along the River Bacchiglione.

Afternoon:

For lunch, visit Osteria Al Bertoldo (Via dei Tadi, 3, 35100 Padova PD, Italy), which offers hearty Italian fare. After lunch, head to Colli Euganei Regional Park (Via Ca' Mureda,

1, 35037 Teolo PD, Italy) for an afternoon of hiking. The park's trails offer stunning views and a chance to immerse yourself in nature.

Evening:

Enjoy dinner at Trattoria Da Ugo (Via dell'Arcella, 20, 35134 Padova PD, Italy), which provides a relaxed atmosphere and delicious local dishes. If you have energy left, consider a leisurely evening walk along the River Bacchiglione to unwind after your adventurous day.

Day 2

Morning:

Start with breakfast at Pasticceria Pinton (Via delle Piazze, 3, 35123 Padova PD, Italy). Then, head to Villa dei Vescovi (Via dei Vescovi, 1, 35030 Luvigliano PD, Italy) for a tour of this stunning Renaissance villa. The surrounding gardens and scenic views are perfect for a morning of exploration.

Afternoon:

For lunch, stop by Ristorante La Folperia (Piazza delle Erbe, 1, 35122 Padova PD, Italy). Afterward, enjoy a boating trip on the River Bacchiglione with Navigazione Bacchiglione

(Lungargine Bassi, 35139 Padova PD, Italy). Relax on the water and take in the city's picturesque scenery.

Evening:

Dine at Ristorante Al Covo (Via Cavour, 12, 35100 Padova PD, Italy), known for its fresh and local ingredients. If you're up for it, visit Parco Montirone (Via Montirone, 35129 Padova PD, Italy) for a tranquil evening walk.

Food and Wine Lover

Day 1

Morning:

Begin your day with a breakfast at Caffè della Piazzetta (Piazza dei Signori, 7, 35139 Padova PD, Italy), which offers a delightful selection of pastries and coffee. Afterward, take a food tour with Padua Food Tours (Via Umberto I, 40, 35122 Padova PD, Italy), where you can sample a variety of local delicacies and learn about Padua's culinary traditions.

Afternoon:

Enjoy lunch at Ristorante Da Giovanni (Via P. del Prato, 14, 35123 Padova PD, Italy), known for its excellent Italian cuisine. After lunch, visit the Mercato delle Erbe (Via delle Erbe, 35122 Padova PD, Italy), a vibrant market where you can explore local produce, cheeses, and wines.

Evening:

For dinner, try Ristorante La Montecchia (Via Montecchia, 10, 35100 Padova PD, Italy), which offers a refined dining experience with a focus on local ingredients. After dinner, visit Enoteca dei Fratelli (Via dei Fratelli, 7, 35100 Padova PD, Italy) for a wine tasting experience.

Day 2

Morning:

Start with a breakfast at Pasticceria Pinton (Via delle Piazze, 3, 35123 Padova PD, Italy). Afterward, visit the Padua Cooking School (Via del Buono, 5, 35100 Padova PD, Italy) for a cooking class where you can learn to prepare traditional Italian dishes.

Afternoon:

Have lunch at Osteria Al Bacco (Via delle Rose, 3, 35100 Padova PD, Italy), which offers a range of Italian specialties. In the afternoon, explore the wine bars around Padua, such as

Vini e Vizi (Via delle Rose, 9, 35100 Padova PD, Italy), known for its excellent selection of local wines.

Evening:

Dine at Ristorante Al 4 Soldi (Via del Santo, 10, 35123 Padova PD, Italy), offering a mix of traditional and contemporary Italian dishes. Enjoy a post-dinner drink at Caffè Minerva (Via dei Mercanti, 8, 35122 Padova PD, Italy) and reflect on your culinary journey.

Budget Traveler

Day 1

Morning:

Begin with a budget-friendly breakfast at Caffè del Museo (Piazza Eremitani, 35121 Padova PD, Italy). Afterward, explore Prato della Valle (Piazza Prato della Valle, 35123 Padova PD, Italy), a beautiful public square that's free to visit and perfect for a leisurely walk.

Afternoon:

For a budget lunch, head to Pizzeria da Pino (Via del Santo, 7, 35123 Padova PD, Italy), which offers delicious and affordable pizza. Spend the afternoon at Parco Montirone (Via Montirone, 35129 Padova PD, Italy), where you can enjoy the park's open spaces and playgrounds without spending a dime.

Evening:

Have dinner at Osteria Al Pomo d'Oro (Via dei Fratelli, 2, 35100 Padova PD, Italy), known for its reasonably priced traditional dishes. Afterward, take a free walk around the University District to soak in the city's atmosphere.

Day 2

Morning:

Start with breakfast at Pasticceria Zanon (Via San Fermo, 2, 35121 Padova PD, Italy), which offers affordable pastries and coffee. Visit the Botanical Garden of Padua (Orto Botanico, Via dell'Orto Botanico, 15, 35123 Padova PD, Italy) for a modest entry fee and enjoy the beautiful plant collections.

Afternoon:

For lunch, try Trattoria da Fabio (Via dei Tadi, 5, 35129 Padova PD, Italy), which offers a budget-friendly menu. After lunch, explore the free museums like the Museo di Padova

(Prato della Valle, 1, 35123 Padova PD, Italy).

Evening:

Dine at Pizzeria Al 4 Soldi (Via del Santo, 10, 35123 Padova PD, Italy) for an affordable and satisfying meal. End the day with a visit to Caffè delle Arti (Piazza delle Erbe, 3, 35122 Padova PD, Italy) for a coffee or a drink in a charming setting.

Returning Visitor Highlights

Day 1

Morning:

Start with a breakfast at Caffè Pedrocchi (Via VIII Febbraio, 15, 35122 Padova PD, Italy), a classic choice for a returning visitor. Revisit your favorite spots like the Basilica of Saint Anthony (Piazza del Santo, 35123 Padova PD, Italy) and the Scrovegni Chapel (Cappella degli Scrovegni, Piazza Eremitani, 35121 Padova PD, Italy).

Afternoon:

For lunch, dine at Ristorante La Folperia (Piazza delle Erbe, 1, 35122 Padova PD, Italy) and enjoy the local flavors. Spend your afternoon revisiting Prato della Valle (Piazza Prato della Valle, 35123 Padova PD, Italy) and enjoy a relaxing stroll through the area.

Evening:

Dine at Ristorante Antico Brolo (Via del Brolo, 1, 35100 Padova PD, Italy) for a special meal. Afterward, take a stroll along the River Bacchiglione and reflect on your favorite memories of Padua.

Day 2

Morning:

Enjoy breakfast at Pasticceria Pinton (Via delle Piazze, 3, 35123 Padova PD, Italy). Revisit any attractions you missed on your previous visits, such as the Palazzo della Ragione (Piazza delle Erbe, 35122 Padova PD, Italy) and the Museo degli Eremitani (Piazza Eremitani, 35121 Padova PD, Italy).

Afternoon:

For lunch, enjoy a meal at Osteria Al Bacco (Via delle Rose, 3, 35100 Padova PD, Italy). Spend your afternoon at the Villa dei Vescovi (Via dei Vescovi, 1, 35030 Luvigliano PD, Italy) or take a leisurely boat ride on the River Bacchiglione with

Navigazione Bacchiglione (Lungargine Bassi, 35139 Padova PD, Italy).

Evening:

End your visit with a special dinner at Ristorante Il Desco (Via San Giovanni, 12, 35121 Padova PD, Italy). If time allows, enjoy a final nightcap at Caffè Minerva (Via dei Mercanti, 8, 35122 Padova PD, Italy) and savor your last moments in this beautiful city.

These itineraries offer a range of experiences to suit different interests and travel styles, ensuring that every visitor to Padua can create lasting memories of this enchanting city.

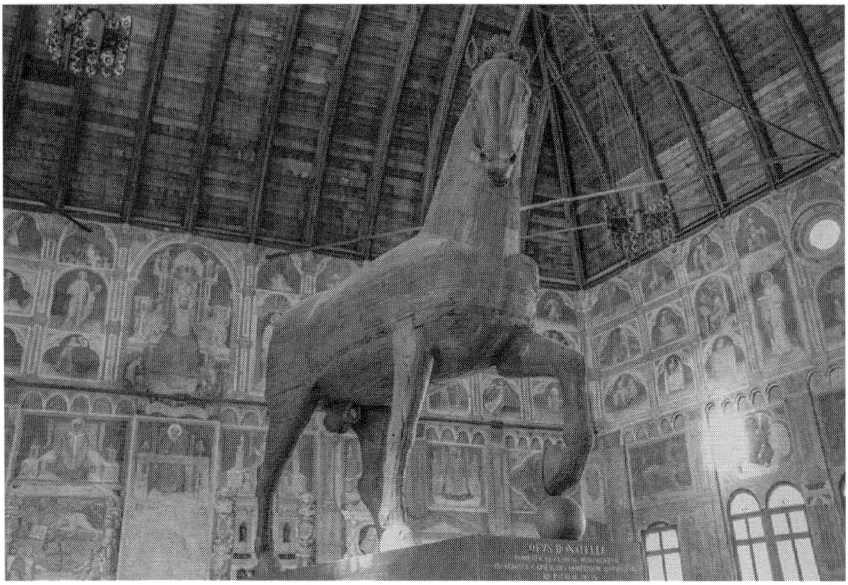

Chapter 11: Practical Information

Visiting a new city, especially one as rich in history and charm as Padua, Italy, can be a thrilling experience. Having a grasp of some practical information can make your stay more comfortable and enjoyable. From health and safety tips to local customs, knowing what to expect can help you navigate your way through this beautiful city with ease. Here's a comprehensive guide to everything you need to know for a smooth trip to Padua.

Health and Safety

One of the first things to consider when traveling is ensuring your health and safety. Padua, like much of Italy, is generally very safe for tourists. However, it's always wise to take a few precautions.

- **Health Care:** Italy has an excellent healthcare system, and Padua is no exception. If you need medical assistance, there are several hospitals and clinics in the city. **The Hospital of Padua** (Ospedale di Padova) is one of the main hospitals, located at Via Giustiniani, 2, 35128 Padova PD, Italy. They offer comprehensive medical services and are well-equipped to handle emergencies. For non-urgent medical needs, you can visit a local pharmacy, known as **"farmacia"** in Italian. Most pharmacists can provide over-the-counter medication and offer advice on minor health issues.

- **Emergency Medical Services:** In case of a medical emergency, you can dial 118 from any phone. This is the emergency number for ambulances and immediate medical assistance in Italy.

- **Travel Insurance:** It's a good idea to have travel insurance that covers health and accident-related expenses. This can provide peace of mind and ensure you're covered for any unexpected situations.

- **Health Tips:** Italy has a warm Mediterranean climate, so stay hydrated, especially during the summer months. Tap water in Padua is safe to drink, but if you prefer bottled water, it's widely available. The city is pedestrian-friendly, but be cautious when crossing streets and watch for bikes and scooters.

Emergency Contacts

Knowing how to reach emergency services and other essential contacts is crucial when traveling. Here are some key numbers and addresses to keep handy during your stay in Padua:

- **Emergency Services (Police, Fire, Ambulance):** 112. This is the European emergency number and can be used for any urgent help.

- **Police Station:** The main police station in Padua is located at Via San Francesco, 35121 Padova PD, Italy. They can assist with any issues related to safety or lost belongings.

- **Consulate:** If you're traveling from outside the EU, it's helpful to know where your country's consulate is located. For U.S. citizens, the nearest consulate is in Milan at Via Principe Amedeo, 2, 20121 Milan MI, Italy.

- **Local Hospital:** Hospital of Padua (Ospedale di Padova), Via Giustiniani, 2, 35128 Padova PD, Italy.

- **Pharmacies:** For any minor health needs or prescriptions, you can visit Farmacia Sant'Antonio, located at Piazza del Santo, 1, 35123 Padova PD, Italy.

It's always a good idea to carry a small card or note with these emergency contacts written down, especially if you're not fluent in Italian.

Local Customs and Etiquette

Understanding and respecting local customs and etiquette can enhance your travel experience and help you interact more comfortably with locals.

- **Greetings and Communication:** Italians are warm and friendly, and a simple greeting like **"Buongiorno"** (Good morning) or **"Buonasera"** (Good evening) is appreciated. When meeting someone, a handshake is common. In more informal settings, close friends and family might greet each other with a kiss on both cheeks.

- **Dining Etiquette:** Meals in Italy are an important part of social life. When dining out, it's customary to wait to be seated, and tipping is not as common or expected as in some other countries. Service charges are often included in the bill. When dining in a restaurant, it's polite to keep your phone on silent and avoid making loud noises. Italians enjoy their meals at a relaxed pace, so don't rush through your meal.

- **Dress Code:** Italians tend to dress well, even for casual outings. It's a good idea to wear smart-casual clothing when dining out or visiting religious sites. For visiting churches and other places of worship, modest attire is required—covering shoulders and knees is a must.

- **Public Behavior:** Italians value personal space but are generally very polite and respectful. In public transportation or public spaces, maintain a quiet demeanor. It's also customary to stand on the right side of escalators to allow others to pass on the left.

- **Shopping and Bargaining:** In most shops and boutiques, prices are fixed, and bargaining is not a common practice. However, in markets or souvenir shops, you might have a bit more flexibility, especially if buying multiple items.

Currency and Banking

Italy is part of the Eurozone, so the currency used is the Euro (€). Here's a quick guide to managing your money while in Padua:

- **Currency Exchange:** You can exchange your currency at banks or exchange offices. In Padua, you'll find currency exchange services at Banca Intesa Sanpaolo, located at Via Roma, 13, 35123 Padova PD, Italy, or at Cambio Veloce in the city center.

- **ATMs:** ATMs are widely available throughout Padua. Look for ATMs with the Cirrus or Maestro logo if you're using an international card. Most ATMs are open 24/7, but be aware of potential foreign transaction fees from your bank.

- **Credit and Debit Cards:** Most restaurants, shops, and hotels in Padua accept major credit and debit cards. However, it's always a good idea to carry some cash for smaller purchases or places that might not accept cards.

- **Banking Hours:** Banks in Padua typically operate Monday to Friday from 8:30 AM to 1:30 PM and might open again in the afternoon from 3:00 PM to 4:00 PM. They are usually closed on Saturdays and Sundays.

Language and Communication

While many Italians in Padua speak English, especially in tourist areas, learning a few basic Italian phrases can enrich your experience and help you interact more easily with locals.

Common Phrases:

- **Hello:** Ciao (informal), Buongiorno (Good morning), Buonasera (Good evening)
- **Please:** Per favore
- **Thank you:** Grazie
- **Excuse me:** Scusi (formal), Scusa (informal)
- **Do you speak English?:** Parla inglese?
- **How much does this cost?:** Quanto costa?
- **Where is the bathroom?:** Dove si trova il bagno?

- **Internet and Communication:** Wi-Fi is widely available in hotels, cafes, and many public areas. If you need to make international calls, consider using apps like WhatsApp or Skype to save on roaming charges.

- **SIM Cards and Mobile Data:** If you're staying for an extended period, you might want to get a local SIM card.

Several mobile operators offer prepaid SIM cards with data packages, such as TIM, Vodafone, and Wind. You can purchase these at mobile shops or convenience stores.

Traveling to Padua is a wonderful adventure, and having this practical information at your fingertips will make your stay more enjoyable and hassle-free. From knowing how to handle emergencies to understanding local customs, being prepared helps you focus on what really matters—exploring and enjoying all that this incredible city has to offer.

Chapter 12: Day Trips from Padua

Padua is such a captivating city, full of history, culture, and charm, but if you find yourself wanting to explore beyond its borders, you're in for a treat. The Veneto region is dotted with delightful destinations that make perfect day trips from Padua. Whether you're drawn to the allure of Venice's canals, the Roman ruins of Verona, or the scenic beauty of the Euganean Hills, there's something for every kind of traveler. Let me take you through some of my favorite day trips that are easily accessible from Padua.

Venice

Ah, Venice! Just a short train ride away, Venice is an enchanting city that needs no introduction. The gondola rides, winding canals, and magnificent architecture make it one of the most romantic and unique cities in the world.

- Getting There: The train ride from Padua to Venice takes about 30 minutes, and you'll arrive at Venezia Santa Lucia Station (Piazzale Roma, 30100 Venezia VE, Italy). Trains run frequently, making it easy to plan a day trip.

- What to See: Start your day at Piazza San Marco (Piazza San Marco, 30124 Venezia VE, Italy), the heart of Venice. Here, you'll find the stunning St. Mark's Basilica (Piazza San Marco, 30124 Venezia VE, Italy), with its opulent mosaics and majestic domes. The adjacent Campanile di San Marco (Piazza San Marco, 30124 Venezia VE, Italy) offers panoramic views of the city.

Next, wander through the Rialto Market (Rialto, 30125 Venezia VE, Italy), where you can soak in the lively atmosphere and pick up some local snacks. A stroll along the Grand Canal provides beautiful views of Venetian palaces and bridges. Don't miss a ride on a vaporetto (water bus) to experience Venice from the water.

For lunch, enjoy a meal at Osteria Al Squero (Dorsoduro, 30123 Venezia VE, Italy), known for its cicchetti (Venetian tapas) and charming atmosphere. In the afternoon, explore the narrow alleyways of Dorsoduro or the Cannaregio district, where you can find quaint shops and peaceful canals.

If you're up for a bit more adventure, visit the Murano and Burano islands, famous for their glassmaking and colorful houses. Regular ferries from Fondamenta Nove (30121 Venezia VE, Italy) can take you there.

Verona

Verona, the city famously associated with Shakespeare's Romeo and Juliet, is a delightful day trip that offers both historical and romantic charm.

- **Getting There:** Verona is about an hour's train ride from Padua. You'll arrive at Verona Porta Nuova Station (Piazzale XXV Aprile, 37138 Verona VR, Italy), which is conveniently close to the city center.

- **What to See:** Begin your exploration at the Arena di Verona (Piazza Bra, 37121 Verona VR, Italy), an ancient Roman amphitheater that still hosts opera performances and concerts. From there, it's a short walk to Juliet's House (Via Cappello, 23, 37121 Verona VR, Italy), where you can see the famous balcony and leave a note to Juliet if you wish.

Next, head to the Piazza delle Erbe (37121 Verona VR, Italy), a bustling square surrounded by medieval buildings, markets, and the Torre dei Lamberti (Piazza delle Erbe, 37121 Verona VR, Italy), which offers a fantastic view of the city. Take a stroll along the Adige River and visit the Castelvecchio (Corso Castelvecchio, 37121 Verona VR, Italy), a historic castle with a museum and picturesque bridge.

For lunch, try Trattoria Al Pompiere (Vicolo Regina d'Ungheria, 1, 37121 Verona VR, Italy) for traditional Veronese dishes. In the afternoon, explore the charming streets of Verona's historic center or visit the Giardino Giusti

(Via Giardino Giusti, 2, 37129 Verona VR, Italy), a beautiful Renaissance garden perfect for a relaxing stroll.

Vicenza

Vicenza, known for its stunning Renaissance architecture, is a gem for architecture enthusiasts and history buffs alike.

- Getting There: Vicenza is about a 30-minute train ride from Padua. You'll arrive at Vicenza Railway Station (Piazzale della Stazione, 36100 Vicenza VI, Italy), which is a short walk from the city center.

- What to See: Start at Piazza dei Signori (36100 Vicenza VI, Italy), the main square surrounded by remarkable buildings designed by the architect Andrea Palladio. The Basilica Palladiana (Piazza dei Signori, 36100 Vicenza VI, Italy) is a masterpiece of Renaissance architecture and offers panoramic views of the city from its terrace.

Next, visit Teatro Olimpico (Piazza Matteotti, 36100 Vicenza

VI, Italy), the oldest surviving indoor theater in the world, also designed by Palladio. Take a stroll along Corso Palladio, where you can admire more of Palladio's works, and explore Villa Rotonda (Viale della Villa, 37, 36100 Vicenza VI, Italy), a short drive from the city center. This villa is another Palladian masterpiece surrounded by beautiful gardens.

For lunch, enjoy a meal at Ristorante La Loggia (Piazza dei Signori, 13, 36100 Vicenza VI, Italy), which offers a delightful mix of traditional and contemporary Italian cuisine. In the afternoon, you can explore the Museo del Risorgimento e della Resistenza (Via del Monte, 36100 Vicenza VI, Italy) to learn more about Italy's history or visit the Giardino Salvi (Piazza dei Signori, 36100 Vicenza VI, Italy), a serene garden perfect for a leisurely walk.

Treviso

Treviso is a charming city often overshadowed by its more famous neighbors, but it has its own unique appeal with its picturesque canals and medieval architecture.

- **Getting There:** Treviso is about a 40-minute train ride from Padua. You'll arrive at Treviso Centrale Station (Piazza Duca d'Aosta, 31100 Treviso TV, Italy), which is close to the city center.

- **What to See:** Begin at Piazza dei Signori (31100 Treviso TV, Italy), the central square lined with historic buildings. Visit the Duomo di Treviso (Piazza Duomo, 31100 Treviso TV, Italy), a beautiful cathedral with an impressive façade and interior. Wander through the Buranelli District, where you'll find charming canals and old houses.

Take a stroll along the Riviera Santa Margherita (Riviera Santa Margherita, 31100 Treviso TV, Italy), a picturesque canal lined with medieval buildings and lively cafes. For a more local experience, visit the Mercato di Treviso (Piazza San Vito, 31100 Treviso TV, Italy) where you can sample local produce and snacks.

For lunch, dine at Antica Osteria Al Botegon (Via Sant'Apollonia, 12, 31100 Treviso TV, Italy) for some traditional Treviso cuisine. In the afternoon, explore the Museo di Santa Caterina (Via Battisti, 31100 Treviso TV,

Italy) which houses an impressive collection of art and artifacts or enjoy a leisurely walk in the Parco degli Alberi Parlanti (Viale della Repubblica, 31100 Treviso TV, Italy), a peaceful park with modern art installations.

The Euganean Hills

For those who love nature and outdoor activities, the Euganean Hills offer a refreshing escape from the city. This volcanic range is known for its natural beauty, charming towns, and therapeutic thermal springs.

- Getting There: The Euganean Hills are easily accessible by car from Padua, located about 20 kilometers southwest. You can drive or take a bus from Padua to the town of Abano Terme (Via Marzia, 5, 35031 Abano Terme PD, Italy), which serves as a good base for exploring the hills.

- **What to See:** Start your day with a visit to Abano Terme, famous for its thermal baths. The Hotel Terme Milano (Viale delle Terme, 91, 35031 Abano Terme PD, Italy) is a popular choice if you want to experience the thermal springs.

Next, explore Montegrotto Terme (Piazza Roma, 1, 35036 Montegrotto Terme PD, Italy), another town known for its spa treatments and beautiful parks. The Parco Urbano Termale (Via delle Terme, 35036 Montegrotto Terme PD, Italy) is a lovely place for a leisurely walk.

If you're into hiking, the Monte Venda (35100 Padova PD, Italy) offers scenic trails and panoramic views of the surrounding countryside. For a more relaxed experience, visit Villa dei Vescovi (Via dei Vescovi, 1, 35030 Luvigliano PD, Italy), a Renaissance villa with beautiful gardens and stunning views.

For lunch, stop by Ristorante La Montecchia (Via Montecchia, 35010 Selvazzano Dentro PD, Italy), which offers delicious local cuisine in a picturesque setting. In the afternoon, visit the Castello di Catajo (Via Catajo, 1, 35020 Battaglia Terme PD, Italy), a historic castle with beautiful gardens and interesting history.

Exploring these nearby destinations from Padua not only offers a diverse range of experiences but also allows you to appreciate the rich tapestry of Italy's Veneto region. Each place has its own unique character and charm, making them well worth the visit. Whether you're seeking cultural immersion, historical exploration, or natural beauty, these day trips provide fantastic opportunities to expand your Italian adventure beyond the city limits of Padua.

Chapter 13: Tips for Sustainable Travel

When you're traveling, it's easy to get swept up in the excitement and sometimes overlook how our choices impact the environment and local communities. As someone who's spent considerable time exploring Padua, I've come to appreciate the beauty of traveling responsibly. Sustainable travel isn't just a trend; it's a way to ensure that the places we love today remain vibrant and intact for future generations. Here's how you can make your trip to Padua more eco-friendly and supportive of local communities.

Eco-Friendly Accommodations

One of the most significant ways to reduce your environmental footprint while traveling is to choose eco-friendly accommodations. Luckily, Padua offers several options where you can rest easy knowing that your stay is more sustainable.

1. Hotel M14

Located at Via degli Scrovegni, 14, 35100 Padova PD, Italy, Hotel M14 is an excellent choice for eco-conscious travelers. This boutique hotel focuses on sustainability by implementing energy-saving measures, such as using LED lighting and solar panels. They also have a comprehensive recycling program and use eco-friendly cleaning products. The staff is knowledgeable about local sustainability initiatives and can offer tips on how to travel responsibly in the area.

2. EcoHotel Bonotto

Situated at Via Monte Grappa, 4, 36100 Vicenza VI, Italy, just a short train ride from Padua, EcoHotel Bonotto is another great option. They are committed to reducing their environmental impact through a variety of practices, including water-saving measures, waste reduction, and the use of renewable energy. Their breakfast features locally sourced, organic products, which means you can enjoy a delicious meal while supporting sustainable agriculture.

3. Relais Santa Corona

While a bit of a drive from Padua, located at Via Santa Corona, 6, 36100 Vicenza VI, Italy, this charming Relais is well worth the visit. They focus on minimizing their ecological footprint through waste management, energy efficiency, and the use of eco-friendly materials in their renovations. Their beautiful gardens are maintained with organic methods, creating a lovely green space for guests to enjoy.

Choosing these kinds of accommodations not only supports businesses committed to sustainability but also sets a positive example for others. It's a simple yet effective way to contribute to the preservation of the beautiful places we visit.

Sustainable Dining

When it comes to dining sustainably, Padua has a growing number of restaurants and cafes that prioritize local, organic, and ethically sourced ingredients. Eating sustainably is not just about choosing the right restaurant but also about being mindful of your consumption habits.

1. Osteria al Cantinon

Located at Via S. Francesco, 24, 35121 Padova PD, Italy, Osteria al Cantinon is a great place to start. They focus on using local and seasonal produce, which reduces the carbon footprint associated with transportation. Their menu features traditional Venetian dishes made with high-quality, sustainably sourced ingredients.

2. Ristorante La Folperia

Found at Piazza dei Signori, 11, 35139 Padova PD, Italy, La Folperia is known for its commitment to using local and organic ingredients. Their menu changes with the seasons, ensuring that you're always enjoying the freshest produce while supporting local farmers. They also have a range of vegetarian and vegan options, catering to a variety of dietary preferences.

3. Gelateria La Romana

For a sweet treat, head to Gelateria La Romana at Via Umberto I, 24, 35129 Padova PD, Italy. This gelateria uses natural ingredients and locally sourced dairy products to create their artisanal gelato. Their commitment to quality and sustainability is evident in every scoop.

When dining out, consider making choices that reduce food

waste. Many restaurants in Padua are open to adjusting portion sizes or providing take-away containers for leftovers. It's also helpful to ask about their sourcing practices to ensure that you're supporting establishments that align with your values.

Responsible Tourism Practices

Being a responsible tourist involves more than just making eco-friendly choices—it's also about respecting the local culture and environment. Here are some practices to keep in mind during your visit to Padua.

1. Respect Local Customs

Padua, like many Italian cities, has a rich cultural heritage. It's important to respect local customs and traditions. For example, dress modestly when visiting religious sites such as the Basilica of Saint Anthony (Piazza del Santo, 35123 Padova PD, Italy). Always follow any rules or guidelines provided at these locations to show respect for the local community.

2. Minimize Plastic Use

Carry a reusable water bottle and shopping bag to reduce plastic waste. Padua has several public water fountains where you can refill your bottle, and many shops are happy to provide paper or reusable bags. By avoiding single-use plastics, you contribute to the cleanliness and sustainability of the city.

3. Support Local Initiatives

Participate in local environmental or cultural initiatives if you have the opportunity. Many cities, including Padua, have community events or conservation efforts that welcome tourist involvement. Whether it's a local clean-up event or a cultural workshop, these activities offer a meaningful way to connect with the community.

4. Use Public Transportation

Whenever possible, use public transportation, walk, or cycle instead of taking taxis or renting a car. Padua has an efficient public transport system, including buses and trains that connect to nearby attractions. This approach reduces your carbon footprint and allows you to experience the city more authentically.

Supporting Local Businesses

One of the best ways to ensure that your travel benefits the local community is by supporting local businesses. Padua has a vibrant array of independent shops, markets, and eateries that rely on patronage to thrive.

1. Visit Local Markets

Padua's markets, such as the Piazza delle Erbe Market (Piazza delle Erbe, 37121 Padova PD, Italy), are perfect for discovering local produce, crafts, and specialties. Shopping at these markets not only supports local vendors but also provides a unique insight into the city's culinary and cultural traditions.

2. Shop at Independent Boutiques

Explore independent boutiques and artisan shops in areas like the Via Roma (Via Roma, 35122 Padova PD, Italy) or Via San Fermo (Via San Fermo, 35122 Padova PD, Italy). These shops often carry handmade goods, unique clothing, and local crafts that make perfect souvenirs while supporting small business owners.

3. Dine at Family-Owned Restaurants

Opt for family-owned restaurants and cafes rather than international chains. Places like Osteria al Cantinon and Trattoria da Nando (Via Palazzina, 11, 35129 Padova PD, Italy) are great examples. These establishments often offer a more authentic dining experience and contribute directly to the local economy.

4. Participate in Local Tours and Workshops

Consider joining local tours or workshops that are run by residents. For instance, a cooking class or a guided walking tour not only enriches your experience but also supports local experts and entrepreneurs.

By incorporating these practices into your travel routine, you can enjoy all the wonders of Padua while making a positive impact on the environment and the local community. Sustainable travel might take a bit more planning and effort, but the rewards are well worth it. You'll leave with not only unforgettable memories but also the satisfaction of knowing that you've contributed to preserving the beauty and culture of the places you visit.

Conclusion

As I close the pages of this travel guide, I find myself filled with a deep sense of satisfaction and joy. Writing about Padua has been a truly rewarding experience, and I'm thrilled to have had the opportunity to share this enchanting city with you. From the ancient charm of its historical sites to the vibrant pulse of its modern life, Padua is a place that captivates the heart and stirs the soul.

I hope that this guide has ignited your wanderlust and equipped you with the knowledge and tools to explore Padua with confidence and curiosity. Whether you're strolling through the lush expanse of the Botanical Garden, marveling at the frescoes of the Scrovegni Chapel, or savoring the rich flavors of local cuisine, my aim has been to provide you with a comprehensive and immersive experience of everything Padua has to offer.

Traveling is more than just visiting new places; it's about making connections, discovering new passions, and creating lasting memories. Padua is a city where history and modernity blend seamlessly, where every corner tells a story, and where every moment is an opportunity for discovery. It's a place that invites you to slow down, savor the little things, and truly engage with its culture and people.

From the lush green spaces of the Euganean Hills to the bustling energy of Piazza dei Signori, I hope you've found inspiration and excitement in these pages. The itineraries crafted for every type of traveler are designed to ensure that your time in Padua is tailored to your interests, whether you're seeking a romantic getaway, a family adventure, or a cultural deep dive.

As you embark on your journey through this incredible city, remember that each experience is a chapter in your own travel story. Embrace the spontaneity of your adventures, engage with the local community, and savor every moment. Padua's charm lies in its ability to offer something unique to every traveler, and I trust that you'll find your own special moments that will make your trip unforgettable.

I've poured my heart and soul into this guide, hoping to offer you a window into the wonders of Padua. If this book has helped enhance your travel experience or provided valuable insights for your journey, I would be incredibly grateful if you could share your thoughts. Your feedback not only helps me improve but also assists other travelers in discovering this beautiful city.

Please take a moment to leave a review on Amazon. Your kind words and honest feedback will not only support my work but also help future readers find the guidance they need to explore Padua with the same enthusiasm and joy. You can find the review section on Amazon.

Thank you for allowing me to be a part of your travel adventure. I wish you an extraordinary journey through Padua and hope that the memories you create will stay with you long after you've left this magical city. Safe travels, and may your explorations be as rewarding and delightful as my own have been.

Warm regards,

— ***Feranmi Samuel***

Appendix

When you're traveling, having the right resources at your fingertips can make all the difference. Whether you're looking for the best restaurants, need to navigate public transport, or want to dive deeper into the local culture, these resources will help you make the most of your time in Padua. Here's a comprehensive guide to useful apps, further reading, and contact information for tourism offices that will enhance your visit.

Useful Apps and Websites

1. TripAdvisor

For reviews and recommendations on hotels, restaurants, and attractions, TripAdvisor is invaluable. It's an excellent way to gauge what other travelers have experienced and find hidden gems. Check it out at www.tripadvisor.com.

2. Rome2rio

When planning your travel routes, Rome2rio is incredibly useful. It helps you figure out how to get from one place to another, whether by bus, train, plane, or ferry. Visit www.rome2rio.com.

3. TheFork

For restaurant reservations and reviews in Padua, TheFork is a fantastic resource. It offers detailed menus, user reviews, and special offers for dining out. Head to www.thefork.com.

4. Google Translate

Language barriers can sometimes be a challenge. Google Translate helps bridge this gap with text, voice, and camera translations. It's a handy tool for communicating with locals and reading menus. Find it at www.translate.google.com.

5. MyTaxi

If you need a taxi or ride-sharing service, MyTaxi (now known as Free Now) can help you find a ride easily. It's perfect for getting around Padua when you're not in the mood to walk. Access it at www.free-now.com.

6. Padova Turismo

For the most accurate and up-to-date information on events, attractions, and activities in Padua, the official tourism website is a great resource. Visit www.padovaturismo.it.

7. Trenitalia

For information on train schedules and tickets, Trenitalia is the go-to source. It's helpful if you plan to explore the Veneto region by train. Check it out at www.trenitalia.com.

8. Uber

Although not as widely used in Italy as in some other countries, Uber is available in Padua and can be a convenient option for getting around. Visit www.uber.com.

9. Yelp

For local restaurant reviews, Yelp provides insights and user experiences that can help you find the best places to eat. It's a good complement to other review sites. Visit www.yelp.com.

Further Reading and References

If you're looking to dive deeper into Padua's history, culture, and attractions, these books and resources will enrich your understanding and appreciation of the city.

1. "Padua and the Veneto" by Michael A. C. Curley

This book provides an in-depth look at the history and attractions of Padua and the surrounding Veneto region. It's a great resource for history buffs and those interested in the cultural heritage of the area.

2. "The Art of Padua" by Elena D'Amico

For art enthusiasts, this book explores Padua's rich artistic heritage, including its famous frescoes and architectural marvels. It's an excellent way to appreciate the city's contributions to art.

3. "Walking Tours of Padua" by David M. Wilson

This guide provides self-guided walking tours of Padua, allowing you to explore the city at your own pace. It's perfect for those who enjoy discovering a city on foot.

4. "Padova: Il Cuore del Veneto" (Padua: The Heart of Veneto)

A local publication that delves into Padua's history, culture, and modern attractions. It's a useful reference for those wanting a deeper dive into the city.

Contact Information for Tourism Offices

For personalized advice and assistance, the local tourism offices in Padua are excellent resources. They can provide maps, brochures, and up-to-date information on events and attractions.

1. Padova Turismo

- **Address:** Piazza delle Erbe, 3, 35121 Padova PD, Italy
- **Phone:** +39 049 820 4550
- **Website:** www.padovaturismo.it

Located in the heart of the city, the Padova Turismo office is a central hub for tourist information. The staff here are friendly and knowledgeable, ready to help with everything from hotel bookings to event recommendations.

2. Tourist Information Office - Padua Railway Station

- **Address:** Stazione FS di Padova, Piazza G. Mazzini, 1, 35131 Padova PD, Italy

- **Phone:** +39 049 820 4367
- **Website:** www.padovaturismo.it

Situated conveniently at the railway station, this office is perfect for travelers arriving by train. It offers a range of services, including information on local transportation and nearby attractions.

3. Veneto Region Tourism Office

- **Address:** Palazzo della Regione, Piazza dei Signori, 1, 35139 Padova PD, Italy
- **Phone:** +39 049 820 4521
- **Website:** www.veneto.eu

This regional office provides broader information on the Veneto region, including Padua. It's a good resource if you're planning to explore beyond the city and need advice on travel and accommodation throughout the area.

4. Tourist Information Desk - Padua Airport (Aeroporto di Padova)

- **Address:** Via G. di Vittorio, 1, 35100 Padova PD, Italy
- **Phone:** +39 049 871 2060

- **Website:** www.padovaairport.it

If you're arriving by air, the information desk at Padua's airport is handy for travelers looking for immediate advice on local transport and accommodation.

With these resources, you'll be well-equipped to navigate Padua and make the most of your visit. Whether you're seeking practical travel tips, cultural insights, or local contacts, these tools will help you create a memorable and well-informed experience.

Padua Map

Scan the QR code below to access a detailed map of the Dolomites. You can zoom in to find specific locations, and the map displays both street and satellite views to help you find your way around the area with ease.